HARRY THE POLIS
IT WISNAE ME . . . HONEST!

. . .

HARRY MORRIS

BLACK & WHITE PUBLISHING

First published 2011
by Black & White Publishing Ltd
29 Ocean Drive, Edinburgh EH6 6JL

1 3 5 7 9 10 8 6 4 2 11 12 13 14

ISBN 978 1 84502 355 3

A CIP catalogue record for this book is available from the British Library.

Typeset by RefineCatch Ltd, Bungay, Suffolk
Printed by CPI Cox & Wyman, Reading

*To my Marion and her continual fight
to raise awareness and find a cure for cancer*

The Highway Code

...

Oot fae the pub, tae the smell o' chips
Chow mein and curry, gies me the pips
Pizza is fine, but it's no' my first choice
So it's intae the chippie, wi' aw the boys
Ah fancy a supper, with a juicy big pickle
Pies, fish or haggis, I'm definitely fickle
Wrapped in the *Herald* or *Evening Times*
Soaking wi' vinegar, a favourite o' mine's
The smell is brill and they taste just great
I've stertit already, 'cause ah cannae wait
Heid doon 'n' eating, my pickle's a stoater
Straight ontae the road, 'n' hit wi' a motor
I'm ten feet in the air, alang wi' my chips
Didnae eat any, 'cause they burned my lips
Noo, I'm deid, 'cause ah didnae look twice
Never ate my pickle, that looked really nice
My fish looked tasty, doused in vinegar 'n' salt
Blootered wi' a motor, but it wisnae his fault
I might just come back, as a kitten or a pup
And when I cross a road, I'll keep my heid up
The moral o' my story, is The Highway Code
Practice makes perfect, when crossing a road!

Contents

. . .

Introduction

. . .

I'm constantly asked the same questions by friends, acquaintances and ex-colleagues: 'Don't you miss the police force, Harry? The harmony, the camaraderie, the laughs with the guys on the shift, the buzz of excitement you feel in your stomach when you're involved in a good bust, culminating with the bad guys getting charged and locked up in a cell?'

My answer to this is always the same. That part of my life has gone; I'm retired from it and you have to move on to the next chapter in your life.

So, as an author with several books published by Black & White, I'm thoroughly enjoying life in my new career.

Here is another collection of my short stories, jokes, anecdotes, tales (and lies) about life. They are not to be taken seriously, but intended to entertain, make you reminisce and bring a smile to your face.

My Harry the Polis series of books is designed to jog your memory, make you laugh and relate a funny story, joke or anecdote to someone who needs to stretch their laughter lines!

Let's face it, we all know some poor bugger who needs a wee laugh now and again! So remember:
'LAUGHTER: THE BEST MEDICINE TO TAKE!'
And best of all, you can never overdose on it either.

Harry

Holy Shit!

. . .

A police firearms officer walked over to a tree during the Raul Moat stand-off and propped up his shotgun against it.

Just then, a gust of wind blew his gun over, causing it to discharge and shoot him in the genitals.

An ambulance was summoned to attend and he was rushed off with sirens blaring to the local Accident and Emergency.

Several hours later, while lying in a hospital bed, he was approached by his doctor who said 'Well officer, I have some good news and some bad news . . . '

'Oh no! I'm going to die . . . Am I going to die doctor? Tell me!'

'No, not at all, in fact, the good news is you're going to be alright. The damage to your genital area was confined to your groin and there was very little internal damage, so we were able to remove all of the buckshot.'

'So what's the bad news then doctor?' Asked the police officer.

'Well the bad news is there was some pretty extensive buckshot damage to your penis and, as a result, I'm going to have to refer you to my brother William.'

'Well, I reckon that isn't too bad, considering.' The police officer replied.

'Is your brother William a top plastic surgeon?'

'Not exactly.' Answered the doctor. 'He plays with the Larkhall Flute Band and he's going to teach you where to put your fingers so you don't pish all over your trouser legs!'

How is Joseph Docherty?

· · ·

A man telephoned London Road Police Office and asked, 'Is it possible to speak to the officer in charge to get an update on a person being detained in custody.'

The operator said, 'Certainly sir. What's the name of the person you are enquiring about?'

The caller replied, 'Joseph Docherty.'

The operator replied, 'Let me put you on hold while I just check with the officer in charge.'

After a few minutes, the operator returned to the phone and said, 'I have good news. I've just been informed that Joseph is being discharged from custody within the next half hour. His details are just being confirmed on the PNC system, after which, he'll be allowed to leave.'

The caller said, 'Oh thanks for that hen. That's good to know. I was so worried. Thanks again for the good news!'

The operator replied, 'You're more than welcome sir . . . Is Joseph your son?'

To which the caller responded, 'No, not at all. It's me! I'm Joseph Docherty and I've been sitting waiting in one of your detention rooms for nearly two hours now and no bugger has bothered their backside to come and tell me a thing about what's happening . . . But now I know . . . Thanks again!'

Away for a Bucket

...

On my way out the other day there, my missus couldn't resist asking me to do some errands whilst I was out.

'Can ye call intae a hardware shop and get me a bucket?'

'Ah bucket? What particular kind would ye like?' I asked.

'Any kind!' She replied. 'It's only a plastic bucket yer buying, no' a motor!'

Armed with my orders from her indoors, I promptly left before she could think of anything else for me to get.

As I drove down the road I saw a hardware shop, so I stopped and went in.

Seeing that the shop assistant was an elderly woman, I decided to have some fun with her and talk in a broken foreign language.

'Yes son, whit can I get ye?' She asked.

'Do you have bucket?' I said.

'A bucket? Whit kind o' bucket would ye like?' She asked.

'Plastic bucket . . . without motor!'

'A plastic bucket without a motor!' She mumbled to herself. 'Aye, jist o'er in the corner there, son.' She replied, directing me towards a display of grey coloured buckets all neatly stacked against a wall.

I stood looking at them for a few moments, prompting her to come over to me and enquire.

'Ur ye awright there, son? Ye look like ye're lost.'

I looked at her and said, 'This is bucket?'

'Aye, that's yer bucket.' She replied.

'Okay, I take bucket.' I said.

The elderly woman reached over and lifted one off the top of the display and, holding it out, she said, 'There ye go son, that'll be £2.99.'

This is where I started to really have some fun.

'Excuse, but do you have red one, thank you?'

'No, I'm sorry son, I've only got grey.' She replied, holding the grey bucket in one hand and extending her other hand out for payment.

'Okay! I take blue one!' I said.

With a puzzled expression on her face, she said, 'I don't have a blue one, I only have grey.' Her voice getting louder.

'But you say you don't have red one?'

'That's right, I don't have a red one but I don't have a blue one either.' At that, she pushed her hand out further, looking for payment. So I continued in this vein.

'Well give to me yellow one, please!'

'Ur you listening, or huv ye a wee problem understaunin' the Queen's lingo? I've telt ye ah only have grey buckets. Look at the display, they're aw grey, noo here, take this!' She said, pushing the grey bucket at me.

'You don't have yellow bucket?' I persisted.

'Naw! I don't have red, blue, yellow, purple, black or any other colour. Ah only have grey buckets!' She blurted out, getting slightly exasperated. 'Noo, dae ye want it, aye or naw?'

'No other colour?' I said.

'Naw, nae other colour, noo here, take it.' She said, forcing the bucket at me.

I looked at her for a moment, as traces of steam began to appear from both her ears and said. 'Okay lady, I will take white one!'

She promptly put the grey bucket back into the display and turned to me and said, 'Read my lips! You . . . oot o' my shop!'

I looked at her with a strained expression and said, 'But I don't understand. I need bucket!'

'Ah know ye dae son, but if I listen tae ye much longer, I'll need a bloody bucket as well. Noo, nae offence, but away ye go tae hell.' She replied. At that, she took hold of my arm and started to lead me to the door.

'Okay! Okay!' I yelled. 'I take grey bucket.'

She immediately stopped, looked at me for a moment, then went back over to the display and picked out the grey bucket again.

'Here!' She said, handing it to me. 'That'll be £2.99!'

As I took possession of the grey bucket, I paused for a moment while fumbling with my money to pay her, 'You take Euro?'

'Naw! Pounds only, none o' that Euro crap.'

As I handed over the money, I couldn't resist asking her again.

'So! You don't have orange bucket?'

At that, she lost it completely, grabbed the bucket back pushed my money into my hand and said, 'That's it, enough's, enough. Get oot ma shop right now, ye're barred!'

With her face getting as red as a beetroot, I had to come clean.

'Woah! Woah! Woah! I'm only kidding ye on hen. It's just a wind-up!' I said.

Whereby, she stopped, looked at me and said, 'Ya big bugger! Are you at it?'

'Aye! I was only joking wi' ye.' I replied.

'Yer jist joking! Well ah hope ye enjoyed the joke, but guess whit, I'm no' joking and you're still barred!' At that she grabbed my arm and guided me to the door.

'Noo get oot ma shop and don't come back!'

Whereby, she promptly slammed the shop door shut.

He's Armless!
...

I saw one of my old police colleagues the other day who was involved in a serious road accident, whereby he had his arm amputated . . . bless him. I shouted over, 'Where are you off to Tommy?'

'To change a light bulb.' He replied.

'That's going to be a bit awkward for you, with only one arm?'

To which he replied in an irate voice.

'Not really. I've still got the frigging receipt, ye sarcastic bastard!'

Anything for You!

. . .

A retired police Commander was sitting with his wife having dinner one evening when he reached across the table, took her hand in his and said, 'Margaret, very soon we will have been married fifty years and there's something I need to ask you. In all these years of married bliss, has there ever been a time when you have been unfaithful to me?'

Margaret looked straight at him, paused for a moment then said, 'Well Alex, I have to be honest with you and answer yes. In all our fifty years together I've been unfaithful to you on three occasions but, in saying that, it has always for a specific reason.'

Alex was obviously upset by his wife's forthright confession and said, 'I never, ever suspected . . . ' Then he thinks for a moment and asks her, 'Can you explain what you mean when you said "specific reasons"?'

Margaret began to explain, 'Well the first time was a few years after we were married and we were about to lose our little house because we were struggling to make the mortgage payments. Do you remember the evening I arranged a meeting with the bank manager and the following day he contacted you and said that our loan would be extended?'

Alex recalled the night she met the bank manager and said, 'Okay! I can forgive you for that. You did it to save our home, but what about the second time?'

Margaret said, 'Right. The second time was when you were very sick and we didn't have the money to pay for the heart surgery you required. Well, I went to see your consultant one night and, if you remember, the very next day, he admitted you and did your surgery with no charge.'

'I remember it well,' said Alex. 'And you did that to save my life, of course I can forgive you for that. But you'll have to tell me about the third time. I need to know in order to put my mind at rest.'

'Alright, alright!' Margaret said. 'Do you remember the time when you decided to run for the position of chairman of the Scottish Police Federation, and you needed to get an extra seventy-three votes?

Well that was the third time!'

Knee Jerk Reaction
• • •

I saw a woman in Glesca wearing a sweatshirt with 'Guess?' on it.

So I said, 'Implants!' And she hit me.

Tam & Senga
• • •

Tam and Senga, a young Glesca couple were walking in the East Kilbride shopping centre with their newborn baby, when they decided to go into the Mothercare Store for a look at some of the latest newborn baby things.

When they came back out they started to walk away, when Senga noticed something different and said, 'Here Tam, that's not our baby.'

Tam replied, 'Shut up Senga and keep walking, it's a better pram than ours!'

Polish it!

. . .

It was a relatively quiet day in the Govan Headquarters' rear charge bar area, so the janitor and a few of the FSO staff were having a clean and tidy up day.

The charge bar was getting a right old spit and polish and, as a result, it was totally gleaming, when a Russian male was brought in as a suspected illegal alien and the duty officer was informed that he spoke in broken English.

He was instructed to empty out his pockets and place all belongings on the custody desk.

He put some coins and keys down and when he took out his bank card, he threw it onto the counter, where it slid along the gleaming custody desk and straight off the other side onto the floor.

Not wishing to appear aggressive, he immediately began apologising.

The duty officer quickly put him at ease.

'It's – okay! - We – polish.'

The bemused, if not confused suspect responded.

'Polish?

No! No! No!

Not Polish.

I'm Russian!'

Nature Boy
...

Early one morning, whilst walking through Rouken Glen Park in Giffnock, my friend Andrew came upon a man hugging a tree with his ear firmly pressed against the tree.

On seeing this he inquired, 'Just out of curiosity mate, what exactly are you doing?'

'I'm listening to the music of the tree.' He replied.

'You're listening to the music of the tree? Are you joking me?' He said.

'Certainly not, would you like to listen for yourself?'

Understandably curious, Andrew said, 'Okay . . . '

Wrapping his arms around the tree, he pressed his ear up against it, whereby the other guy slapped a pair of handcuffs on his wrists and promptly relieved him of his wallet, watch and car keys, after which, he stripped him of all his clothes and left him naked.

Andrew called out for help, but to no avail.

However, after about two hours another nature lover out for a morning walk in the park strolled by, saw Andrew in the nude, handcuffed to the tree and asked, 'What the hell happened to you, pal?'

Andrew related the whole terrible story to his rescuer, about what had taken place and when he'd finished telling his story, the other guy shook his head in sympathy, before he casually walked around the tree behind him, kissed him gently behind the ear and whispered, 'This just isn't going to be your day pal, or should I say, sweetheart . . .'

Christmas Quiz

. . .

It is near the Christmas break at Tulliallan Police College and Donnie Henderson junior and the rest of the police cadets have handed in all their class work for the day and there is really nothing more for them to do but watch the clock.

The cadets are restless and desperate to get home. So the sergeant decides to have an early dismissal quiz with some famous quotes and said, 'Whoever answers the questions I ask first and correctly can leave the college early today.'

Donnie junior says to himself, 'Good, I want to get out of here toot sweet. I'm smart, so I'm a certainty to answer a question.' The sergeant opened his book of famous quotes and asked, 'Who said, "Four Score and Seven Years Ago"?' Before Donnie junior can open his mouth, Betty Moore shouts out, 'Abraham Lincoln.'

'That's correct Betty' Said the sergeant. 'You can leave.' Donnie junior is mad that Betty answered the first question.

'Next question. Who said during his Civil Rights Speech, "I Have a Dream"?'

Before Donnie can even guess who, Laura Turner shouted out, 'Martin Luther King.'

'Correct Laura.' He said. 'You too can go.' Young Donnie is seething and even angrier than before.

'Okay ladies and gents, next question, who said, "Ask not, what your country can do for you, bu . . ."'

Before he can even finish the famous quote, Marion Davren interrupts him, 'John F. Kennedy.'

'That's right Marion, well interrupted, you may also leave.'

Donnie junior has steam coming out of his ears that he has not been able to answer any of the questions before a female.

When the sergeant turns his back for a moment Donnie junior mumbles, 'I wish all these bitches would keep their big mouths shut!'

The sergeant turns around and asked: 'Now who was it that said that?'

Quick as a flash young Donnie junior shouted out, 'Tommy Sheridan. Now can I go sergeant?'

Imitation Love

• • •

Big Donnie was telling me that when he was on his own for a while and yearned for some female company, he bought himself a blow up doll but when he started dating a new girlfriend, he had to let her down slowly!

Back To Front

...

Two anti-terrorist security officers from Strathclyde Police arrived late for an important seminar being held at a hotel in London. They were immediately directed to the sixth floor, where the entire seminar assembly was awaiting their arrival.

Armed with several shoulder bags containing files and laptops, they hurriedly entered the hotel elevator. Perspiring profusely from their efforts, they comported themselves as the elevator went up. On arrival at their destination, the elevator stopped and a recorded voice announced, 'Welcome to the sixth floor, doors opening'.

Both police officers paused while awaiting the doors to open . . . Moments later, anxiety took over as the doors remained firmly shut.

The officers took action by dropping their bags to the floor and trying to prise open the doors with their finger-nails and even a pen, whilst banging on the doors with their fists, to raise attention of their plight, but to no avail. Then, a second announcement was heard, 'Doors closing' . . . But the doors in front of them still remained firmly shut.

Panic took over as they pressed the emergency elevator button several times. Suddenly, loud sniggering and laughter was heard coming from behind them. Both officers slowly turned around to see a lobby filled with hotel guests, all waiting patiently to enter the lift! . . . Ooops!!

Spoil Sport

. . .

Nigel Preston, an underwear designer from London University, has designed a new bra in competition with our very own Michelle Mone and Ultimo.

This new design by Nigel holds a woman's breasts firmly. It stops them from juggling around; bouncing up and down and even prevents the nipples from pushing through the fabric when cold weather sets in.

At a news conference, while on tour in Glasgow city centre, to launch his latest design and get a reaction, a group of male protesters calling themselves, 'BOOBS' (Boys Only Ogle Big Stoaters) with placards displaying, 'GET THEM OOT FOR THE BOYS' physically dragged Mr Preston outside onto the Buchanan Street precinct and proceeded to kick pure shit out of him.

As they say . . . If it's not broken . . . Don't fix it!!

'Ye cannae beat a peaceful protest to get your point across!'

An Apple a Day

. . .

Apparently Apple have scrapped plans to bring out a new iPod for children. They feel the new name 'iTouch Kids' might not go down too well as a product name.

ESSO

. . .

Tam McEwan was a serving Glesca cop whose nickname was ESSO (Eats, Sleeps, Shits Overtime) and who'd transferred from the city of Glasgow police to Argyll & Bute police.

About 1.30am one Sunday morning, a call came into Dunoon Police Office complaining about a noisy party being held in Lochgoilhead.

Tam was working in the area and was instructed to attend the call.

However, the shift sergeant was well aware of Tam's ability to stretch out an incident and in doing so, create for himself some unplanned overtime, so he decided to try and solve the noisy party problem himself over the phone.

Firstly, he contacted the householder and explained that there had been a complaint about the noise from the party and advised him to turn the music down.

The party hosting householder, consumed with large amounts of alcohol which caused him to chance his arm said.

'Ye're calling me fae Dunoon ye say?'

'That's correct.' Replied the sergeant.

'Well that's a helluva long way away. Whit ye gonnae dae if I don't turn my music down?' He asked with a cocky attitude.

'Trust me son. It'll surprise you what I can do from here.' The sergeant said, using his best bluff.

'Like whit? He replied.

'I'll do something you wouldn't believe!' The sergeant said, still bluffing.

'Let's see ye dae it then . . . Go on, dae it! A dare ye!' Replied the cocky householder.

Just at that moment . . . lo and behold, there was an unexpected electric power cut to the area.

At that, there was a moments pause, when the surprised householder could be overheard by the sergeant talking to his party guests, 'For fuxsakes . . . the big bastert has just cut my electricity power off . . . Fae Dunoon!'

'Fae Dunoon?' Asked a guest. Surprised by this.

'Aye! Fae bloody Dunoon!'

At which point the sergeant took the opportunity to issue a stern warning to the householder. 'Right, are you listening, that's it, party over, now get to your beds, before I'm forced to do something else you'll really regret.'

'Okay big man, okay! The party's over, we're going tae bed . . . I'm sorry about that, okay?' at that the phone went down.

As for Tam, still en route to the call, by this time, he was in a radio blackspot area and never heard the cancellation from the sergeant for his call, so he still managed to wangle his overtime hours.

No' bad eh!?

Ear, Nose & Throat

• • •

A policewoman booked an appointment to see the chief medical officer and on attending his surgery she said, 'Doctor, you have to help me . . . I've got this terrible problem; you see I can't stop passing wind. I'm farting all the time, the only saving grace for me is they're silent and don't smell.

'As a matter of fact, I've farted at least half a dozen times since I've sat down in your room while talking to you.'

The police doctor sat there listening intently to everything she had to say, then began writing out a prescription and handing it to her, he said, 'Here, take these and come back and see me after seven days.'

At that, she left his surgery and after seven days, returned to see him again.

'Doctor, you need to help me!' She pleaded again. 'Things are going from bad to worse. I'm still farting like a trooper, and they're still silent, but now they stink like hell. You must do something for me!'

Then she pauses for a moment before asking, 'By the way doctor, what were those pills meant to do that you prescribed for me?'

To which the police doctor replied, 'Oh don't worry, those pills were just to sort out your sinus condition and now that they appear to have cleared your nasal passage and your sense of smell is back, I think we'll work on your hearing problem next.'

Donnie's Dilemmas

...

I contacted my old friend Donnie Henderson, regarding an ex-colleague's retirial party. 'What's the dress code Harry?' He asked me.

So I innocently told him, 'Just dress to kill, Donnie.'

Trust Donnie to take it too far and turn up in a white turban, black beard and wearing a large backpack. Not exactly what I had in mind.

During the evening drinking session, I mentioned to Donnie, that Christmas was on a Friday this year. Donnie replied, 'Well let's just hope it's not on the thirteenth, cause that'll be really unlucky!'

Donnie was telling me he'd just hired an Eastern European cleaner and it took her four hours to hoover the carpets in his house. It turns out she was a Slovak.

Donnie was saying that two women called at his door doing a survey on what bread he ate, when Donnie said he preferred white, they gave him a lecture for thirty minutes on the benefits of eating brown bread . . . He reckons they were 'The Hovis Witnesses'!

All winter, with the heavy snow falling, Donnie was saying all his wife has done, is constantly look through the lounge window. If the weather gets any worse, he reckons he's going to have to let her back in.

Donnie was telling me he arrested a male and charged him with murder for killing a man with sandpaper.

Apparently, the accused's defence was, 'He only intended to rough him up a bit.'

After a heavy night of lots of alcoholic drinks at a party, followed by some wild sex, Donnie woke up the very next morning to find himself in bed beside a really ugly woman.

That's when he realised he had made it home safely.

After years of research, Donnie has discovered what makes a woman happy . . . Nothing!

On a lighter note, Donnie told me he'd received his quarterly bill from Scottish Water for £180.

That's a helluva lot of money, considering Oxfam are advertising that they can supply an entire African village for just £2 a month. He's thinking of changing supplier to them!

Finally, Donnie received an email today from a bored Glesca housewife, who was looking for some hot action!

So he sent her his ironing over. That should keep the bitch busy.

Bootiful

· · ·

It was with great sadness that I learned about the recent death of Bernard Matthews, the well known turkey farmer with the TV advert catchphrase, 'It's bootiful, really bootiful!'

Apparently, it was his last wishes to be cremated at Gas Mark 6 for three hours, with his loving flock of 'bootiful' turkeys forming a gobbling guard of honour while looking on.

Christmas will never be the same!

Direct Line

• • •

My friend Jay Drennan is a Federal Prison officer in America and sent this story to me. It took place in Charlotte, North Carolina and refers to a 'smart arse lawyer' who purchased a box of very rare and expensive Cuban cigars and then insured them against, among other things, fire.

Within a month of having smoked his entire stockpile of these rare cigars, the lawyer filed a claim against the insurance company.

In his claim, the lawyer stated the cigars were lost 'in a series of small fires'! Obviously, the insurance company refused to pay out, citing the reason that the insured had consumed the cigars in the normal fashion.

However, the lawyer sued them and WON!

(Now keep reading, 'cause you'll love the next part!)

Delivering the ruling, the judge agreed with the insurance company that the claim was indeed frivolous but he also stated that nevertheless, the lawyer held a policy with the company which had warranted that the cigars were insurable and also guaranteed. They were insured against fire and without the company defining what is considered to be an unacceptable explanation for 'fire', so the company were duly obligated to pay out the claim.

Rather than endure a lengthy and costly appeal process, the insurance company accepted the ruling of the court and paid $15,000 to the lawyer for his loss of the cigars that perished in the 'fires'.

Now for the best part.

After the lawyer cashed the cheque, the insurance

company had him arrested and charged with twenty-four counts of arson!

With his own insurance claim and testimony from the previous case being used against him, the lawyer was found guilty and convicted of intentionally burning his insured property and was given a custodial sentence of two years in prison and fined a whopping $24,000.

This true story won First Place in last year's Criminal Lawyers Award contest.

Now let's be honest, it could only happen in America!

Translator

. . .

On holiday recently in Spain I saw a sign outside a surgery saying,

'English speaking doctor'.

I thought what a good idea, why didn't we think of that in our country!

Use a Typist

...

The civilian officer in charge of the clothing supplies for the police office civilian assistants received a large supply of the new look black police t-shirts to his clothing store.

Desperate to start distributing them immediately, due to the amount of space they were taking up in his storeroom, he couldn't be bothered dictating a memo for the typist. So to notify the various offices in the area, he decided to type out his own instructions with details of the swap over and collection. Unfortunately, he didn't use spell check on his word processor and as a result his memo ended up slightly obscured from what he actually meant to say.

'Would all force station officers and departmental assistants please call at the Police Headquarters Clothing Store, within the next three days with your old shits and we will supply you with a nice new one. Failing your appearance at the stores, we will send you a supply through despatches.'

Sounds a bit smelly to me, all this shit going about in the mail!

The Phone Call

. . .

Several cops had arranged a shift golfing tournament and were in the locker room of the golf club getting changed, when a mobile phone on a bench rang and one of the cops, putting on his golf shoes, engaged the hands-free speaker function and answered it.

Everyone else in the locker room stopped what they were doing to listen in to his conversation.

'Hellooo!'

A woman's voice responded. 'Hi honey, it's just me. Are you at the club yet?'

'Yes I'm here.' He replied.

'Well I'm just calling you to say I'm at the shops now and I've found this beautiful tan suede coat. It's in the sale at only £900. Is it alright if I buy it? It really is gorgeous and I look great in it.'

'Why not darling! Just go ahead if you like it that much.'

'Oh thanks, honey.'

'No problem!' He replied.

'Oh and honey, I passed by the Jaguar garage on my way here and I saw the new models in the showroom. There's one there I really loved.' She said, pushing her luck.

'How much is it?' He asked her.

'It's only £72,000, but it looks fabulous.' She replied.

'Well okay, but for that price, tell them you want it with all the extras included.'

'Why honey, you are in a good mood. I must have been better than I thought this morning!'

'Well you should know, darling!' He replied.

'I'm glad you said that honey, because I've one more thing to ask you.' She said sheepishly.

'Well you might as well ask. Best to strike while the going's good.'

'Okay honey, here it is. I was just talking to Mhairi at Countrywide Properties and she was telling me that the house I really wanted last year is back on the market and get this, the owners have only gone and reduced the price and are now asking £675,000 for it.'

'Sounds like a steal darling. Why don't you call them up and make an offer of £650,000. They'll probably take it. If not, we can go the extra twenty five grand if it's what you really want.' He said confidently.

'Oh thank you my honey. I'll see you later! Oh I love you so much!'

'Alright darling, bye for now! And I love you, too.' At that, he hangs up.

All his police colleagues within the locker room were staring at him in astonishment, with their mouths wide open at what they had just heard, when he turned around to face them all and asked, 'Does anybody know whose mobile phone this is?'

Britain's Constitution
· · ·
They keep talking about drafting a Constitution for Iraq . . .

Why don't we just give them ours? It was drawn up by a lot of really smart guys, who put a lot of thought into it over a long period of time and it has worked for centuries and after all, we're not using it anymore . . . Why not!

Too Hot!
· · ·
I stepped out of the shower the other day and it was just too hot to wear clothes. I said to my wife, 'What do you think the neighbours would say if I went outside into the garden and cut the grass in the nude?'

To which she replied, 'Probably that I married you for your money!'

Bumper Sticker
· · ·
I thought this sticker was quite topical.

'If you can read this, then thank your teacher and, since it's in English, thank the British Army.'

Bargain Galore

. . .

This is a take on one of the many 'junk emails' that everyone cannot escape receiving during this time of year and as you can tell by the language and spelling . . . it's probably a company in Saltcoats!

Hullo fellow bargain hunter and wellcome to my grate nue site, www.fillupwithmanybargain.com So many bargain, their a steel. Just donut tell polis . . . ha ha.

We offer top brang names, such as Lackoste, Cristin Door, Nice, Burburry and Tifanny . . . many uther bargain online to order, like Deasel, Uggly, Jimmy Shui, Monte Blank and Caterpillar boots to fit every pear of feat, pear of feat, pear of feat . . . My staff of shoplifters, sorry, shop fitters are busy clearing shelves of anything . . . to sail!

Beat the VAT and pay under the counter prices . . . Cash only! Luvly jubbly bargain, with many other discunts to see . . . just coming straight off the back of the lorry and in the back door as we speak, handcuffies and sea frew panties with thrill from Ann Sumer shop in east kilbride . . . and Boots . . . condums bags . . .

Velly rubbery!

Good bargain, come kwikkly.

Everyone a genuine fake . . . garinteed, or yer money back!

. . . NOT!

The Marriage

...

A retired police officer met a beautiful blonde lady on the internet and instantly struck up a relationship and decided he wanted to marry her.

She said, 'But we don't know anything about each other.'

'That's alright,' He replied, 'we can learn about one another as we go along, it'll be fun.'

So she agreed to be wed and off they went on a honeymoon to a very nice Spanish resort.

One morning they were lying by the pool, when he got up off of his sun lounger, climbed up to the ten metre diving board and did a two and a half tuck, followed by three rotations in the pike position, at which point he straightened out and cut the water like a knife.

After a few more demonstrations, he came back and lay down on the towel. She said, 'That was incredible darling!'

'Thank you!' He replied, 'but I used to be a police diving champion and I competed for the police all around Europe.

You see, I told you we'd learn more about each other as we went along.'

A few moments later, she got up from her sun lounger, jumped into the pool and began swimming lengths.

After seventy-five lengths of the pool, she climbed out, lay down on her towel and was hardly out of breath.

'That was unbelievable sweetheart! Don't tell me, let me guess. Were you some kind of Olympic endurance swimmer?'

To which she replied, 'No! I was a prostitute in Glasgow and used to work both sides of the River Clyde.'

Seafood Platter

...

A man reported his wife had gone missing whilst swimming in a loch in Scotland.

The police immediately organised divers to make a thorough search of the loch while the husband spent the next few hours worrying about what could have happened to her.

The following morning the man was awakened by a knock at the front door and he opened it to find an old sergeant and a young constable standing there.

The sergeant said, 'I'm sorry to inform you sir, but we have some news for you. Unfortunately, it's very bad news, but in saying that, I also have some good news and maybe even some more good news.'

'Well!' Said the man, 'I suppose I'd better sit down and hear the bad news first.'

The sergeant said, 'I'm really sorry to have to tell you this, but your wife is dead. Young Dickson here found her lying submerged in about ten metres of water amongst some rocks. He managed to get a rope around her legs and we pulled her to the surface, but unfortunately, it was too late, she was dead.'

The man was naturally distressed to hear this news about his wife and passed out with the shock of it all but after a few moments, he pulled himself together and asked what the good news was.

The sergeant said, 'Well, when we pulled your wife up to the surface, there were quite a few really good sized crayfish and several nice crabs attached to her body, so we've brought you over your share.' At that, he handed the grieving husband a carrier bag with a couple of very nice crayfish and two or three crabs in it.

'Gee wiz officers. They're bloody beauties right enough. I guess it's an ill wind and all that . . . So what's the other piece of good news you have for me?'

'Well!' The sergeant said, 'If you fancy going for a quick trip, me and young Dickson here get off duty at around 11 o'clock and we're planning to drive back over there and pull her up again!'

She's Electric
• • •

Big Donnie was telling me he met this beautiful female for the first time recently and had amazing sex with her. The sparks were flying everywhere.

He reckons that owning a Taser Gun is definitely money well spent!

Let There Be Light!

· · ·

A retired cop goes for a check up to the doctors and all of his tests come back with normal results for man of his age.

The doctor says, 'David, everything looks good. How are you doing mentally and emotionally? Are you at peace with God?'

David replied, 'Suffice to say, God and I are very close. For example, he knows my eyesight is failing, so he's fixed it for me when I get up in the middle of the night to go to the bathroom, POOF! I don't have to grope about in the dark for the light switch, the light goes on automatically for me, and when I'm finished, POOF! The light goes off automatically.'

'Wow! That's incredible David,' replied the doctor.

Later that day, the doctor called David's wife.

'Hi Jean! (She was a thoroughly good cleaner) 'Just a quick call to let you know that David is doing fine but I had to call you because I'm in awe of his strong belief that he has a close relationship with God. Is it true that he gets up during the night and POOF! The light automatically goes on in the bathroom, and when he's finished, POOF! The light goes off?'

To which Jean responded, 'Oh my God! The old bugger's peeing in the bloody fridge again!

What'll it Be!

· · ·

Tam McEwan was a City of Glesca boy, through and through, and it was quite entertaining for the cops in the 'County' areas when he transferred out to their area, prior to almagamation and they realised he wasn't joking about his lack of country knowledge.

However, give Tam his due, he was very soon into the swing of things and I have to admit that some of his city dodges helped the county cops too.

On a winter's night, about 8pm. Tam was driving and Ricky Gault was observer. As they drove along the A815 north of Dunoon alongside Loch Eck, just short of the Coylet Inn, an animal appeared from the bushes and bounced across the road about 200 yards away in front of them. I say bounced, because it was a wallaby.

Ricky being the local cop said to Tam, 'Did you see that?' As there had been no reaction from Tam as to its presence on the road.

'No, whit?' Replied Tam.

'A wallaby! It was a wallaby!' Said Ricky.

'Aye right!' Replied Tam. 'Whit's a frigging wallaby?'

'A marsupial!' Replied an excited Ricky.

'Whit the hell is a marsupial?' asked Tam.

This description appeared to confuse Tam, so Ricky compromised for his Glesca colleague and said, 'A wee kangaroo!'

Tam turned the police van, parked at the side of the road and waited for a few moments and sure enough, it bounded back across the road in front of them and up into the woods.

'Granny' Smith, the shift sergeant was for breathalysing both of them, when he heard the story.

However, this brief encounter with the wallaby obviously had a profound effect on Tam, for only a few years later, he emigrated to Australia and joined the Perth police.

Either that or, he was just crap at geography and meant to join Perth police in Tayside Scotland!

St James Church

. . .

My mother's wee church in Pollok were holding a fund raising Car Boot Sale and the minister, who is renowned for his witty remarks, handed out a flyer about it to the chuch congregation as they left last Sunday.

It read, 'Please don't forget the Car Boot Sale. It's a chance to get rid of all those old, useless things that are not worth keeping around the house anymore . . . Don't forget to bring your husbands!'

And my particular favourite notice posted outside:

'Weight Watchers will meet at 6pm at the St James Church.

Would all new members please use the large double door at the side entrance.'

Now for me, that'll certainly boost their confidence at the weigh-in!

A Glasgow Endearment

. . .

I suppose being an author, writing a book series and performing stand-up shows around the country, makes my face recognisable to some people. Add to that an article published in the *Scottish Sun* with an updated picture of me, then it is inevitable that someone is bound to notice you.

My particular time came about a few days ago after the *Scottish Sun* article had come out and I was taking my elderly mother shopping in her local Morrison's Supermarket.

Just as we were leaving the canteen area after our lunch, a middle aged man approached, pointed his finger at me, cocked his head to one side and said, 'Hey big man! Wis that a story about you in the *Sun* the other day there wi' yer mugshot?'

Delighted that he had even bothered to read the article, never mind recognise me by my picture, I said, 'Yes, it was me.'

At that a broad smile broke out across his face and he offered his hand as a gesture to shake with mine.

'Ah knew it!' He said, before repeating. 'Ah jist knew it! Ah opened the paper, saw yer coupon looking straight oot at me and said tae my wee maw, see him maw . . .

Ah know that big bastard!'

Sausages!
...

I thought I'd heard them all but recently a case was thrown out of the court because it was deemed to be absolutely ridiculous, and rightly so.

The case in question was a criminal charge of assault against a male accused of allegedly hitting a woman in the face with a flying sausage.

The accused had been originally charged with assault, causing actual bodily harm, as a result of injuries sustained by the female victim.

Don't laugh just yet, because this isn't a joke . . . It's true . . . Honest!

Apparently they were both at a house party when, during the buffet, a food fight broke out and she was the recipient of a flying chipolata sausage to the face, thrown by the accused.

Let's face it; we've all been to parties where the buffet was cold, crap and usually made up by a favourite auntie and her pal! Am I right?

To make matters worse for the accused, the female changed her story and stated that it might even have been . . . wait for it (drum roll) . . . a KFC chicken drumstick that was thrown causing her injury.

Now this took place, as you might have guessed already, in England. I emphasise that because it would never have been given the light of day in Glasgow, where at least nine out of ten households have been blootered in the face weekly with the entire contents of a pan 'fry up'.

Yes, I have to own up to having been decorated on more

than one occasion with sausage, bacon, egg, tattie scone and fried tomato . . . whilst still attached to the plate, but a sausage by itself! Give me a break hen!

Some Friday nights, my wife has phoned the local Chinese restaurant for a carry out chicken curry with fried rice, just to see what it looks like over me. Personally, I prefer lemon chicken.

I can also confess to having worn at one time or another several late-night TV dinners, on my arrival back from the pub, followed by the odd apple tart and custard, or strawberry yoghurt.

Drumstick, huh! In Glesca, I've sampled the whole chicken.

These women down south have no idea about marital life, or a bloody good house party.

Up in Glesca, I was sent to a call where a woman threw a 'Glesca salad' all over her husband.

I didn't think that much of it, until I was re-directed and instructed to attend the Western Infirmary Burns Unit. It was there I learned that a 'Glesca salad' was a nickname for a pan of roasting hot chips and he had sustained some serious burns to his face and body.

You don't get scarred for life with a bit of feta cheese from a Greek salad.

With some couples, it's an essential part of marital bliss and a game that the entire family can play! And then make up again later.

Being born in the Plantation area of Glesca and reared in tenements of Drumchapel, my mother would have been charged on a daily basis by the polis. She was always firing pieces of butter and jam out of our three storey high window at me and my brothers and sisters.

It was the only way we got fed. Catching the tea was another matter!

With three brothers and two sisters, my mother was like a Frisbee thrower, with slices of plain bread flying around the 'Drum' like UFOs.

God forbid if she missed her aim and struck an unsuspecting wean on the napper . . . She'd have been libelled with attempted murder, or aggravated assault, having coated the bread with butter and jam.

And toast would have definitely carried a more serious charge.

But fortunately, we Scots are blessed with more common sense.

Finally, I once attended a Friday night incident in a house where the man had hit his wife with a supper.

On entering the house, he said, 'Check oot her coupon. She's got a face like a fish supper . . . It's all chips!'

Help is Near

· · ·

Loved this bit of grafitti I saw recently on the rear of a large truck.

'Don't let depression get you down, contact the Samaritans for some help!' . . . I think I know what they meant.

That's Life

. . .

Several years ago when my son Scott was about twelve years old, I thought I would ask him if he knew about the birds and bees.

'No! And I don't want to know.' He then became quite upset. 'Promise me you won't ever tell me!' He pleaded.

You can imagine how confused I was at hearing this and seeing my son's reaction. What was wrong with him, I thought. So I asked him.

'Well, it's like this dad, when I was six, you gave me the, "There's no Easter Bunny" speech.

'Then when I was seven, you told me there was no such thing as the Tooth Fairy.

'I had just turned nine when you reliably informed me, there was no Santa Claus and ruined my Christmas!

'And last year, you told me there was no more "Flaming Flumes" because the Time Capsule had disappeared like a rocket along with Guy Fawkes on the 5 November.

'So if you're going to tell me now that grown-ups don't have sex anymore, I'll have nothing left to live for!'

A bit over the top there son!

Swap Over

...

I've came up with a way of giving our Old Aged Pensioners a better retirement life.

It is so simple, why haven't we, our government, thought of it before?

What we do is, round up all of our senior citizens and drive them up to the nearest HMP (Her Majesty's Prison) and swap places with the criminals, then convey the criminals to the nursing homes. This way, all the senior citizens would enjoy the benefits of access to hot, clean showers, learn new hobbies such as painting and sculpture and participate in daily exercises.

They'd also be able to take advantage of the health system with unlimited free prescriptions, dental checks and medical treatment and would receive payment for staying the course instead of paying it out to have the benefits given to them.

They would have constant video monitoring, so they could be helped instantly, if they tripped and fell over or needed general assistance.

Their bedding would be washed twice a week, and all clothing would be ironed and returned to them.

A 'senior citizen carer guard' would make checks on them every thirty minutes and serve them their meals and snacks to their furnished cell.

They would have regular family visits in a luxury suite built for that purpose.

They would have unlimited access to a library, weight room, spiritual counselling, pool area and educational courses of their choice.

Simple clothing, shoes, slippers, pyjamas and legal aid assistance and advice would be freely available to them all, on request.

With private and secure rooms for all, with an outdoor exercise yard, with well maintained, mature gardens with pathways and family picnic areas with BBQs.

Every senior citizen could have a computer, DVD player, plasma screen TV, radio and regular daily telephone calls.

There would be a board of directors to hear any complaints, and the guards would have a code of conduct that would be strictly adhered to at all times ... 'The senior citizens know best!'

Over at the 'convicted criminals' nursing home accommodation, they could enjoy the luxurious life of an OAP and would be served up cold food at meal times, be left for hours on end alone and unsupervised, needing the toilet.

All lights would be switched off at 8pm, and showers would only be available once a week, on request and if there was enough hot water.

There would be no electrical devices, such as TVs, unless purchased by themselves along with a valid TV licence.

They would each be assigned a tiny room and pay £800 per month for the privilege of living there, with no hope of ever getting out.

Now! What do you say we vote on that one readers!

I'm Here
· · ·

Is it just me, or does anyone else find it quite amazing that during the 'mad cow disease' epidemic, the government in power at the time, could trace a single cow, born on a farm in Truro almost three years ago, straight to the barn where it slept in the county of Cornwall!

Not only that, they could even trace her calves to their stalls.

But they are unable to locate over 200,000 illegal immigrants wandering around aimlessly in our country.

Call me cynical, but maybe we should supply them each with a cow!

Safe Sex
· · ·

My colleague Donnie Henderson was telling me his son came home the other night and said, 'Hey Dad, I've just had sex with the next door neighbour's seventeen-year-old daughter!'

Thinking about the number of STD cases resulting from casual sex, Donnie said, 'I hope you covered up!'

To which his son replied, 'Of course I did. I wore my black balaclava!'

Good Joke

•••

I just love the odd joke like this that comes along to me via an email from an ex-colleague . . . I think you'll like it too!

A husband takes his young wife to play her first game of golf.

He sets her up with the proper stance and position to hit her first drive from the tee. Unfortunately his wife promptly hacked the shot to the right, straight through the window of the biggest house parallel to the course.

The husband cringed, 'Gee wiz Norma, I warned you to be careful! Now we'll have to go up there, find the owner, apologise and see how much your lousy drive is going to cost us.'

So they both walked up to the house and knocked on the front door, where a welcoming voice greeted them and said, 'Please, come on in.'

When they opened the door they immediately focussed on the damage that was caused with glass scattered all over the floor, and a broken antique bottle lying on its side near the pieces of window glass.

A man, reclining on the sofa asked, 'Are you the people that broke my window?'

'Uh . . . yes, sir. We're really sorry about that.' The husband replied.

'No apology is necessary . . . Actually, I would like to thank you . . . You see, I'm a genie, and I've been trapped in that bottle for a thousand years and now that you've released me, I'm allowed to grant you three wishes.

I will permit you to have one wish each, but if you don't mind, I would appreciate it, if I can keep the last one for myself.'

'Wow, that's great!' The husband said, rubbing his hands together and looking at his wife. 'I'll go first.'

He pondered for a moment and then blurted out, 'My wish is to have a million dollars, each and every year for the rest of my life.'

'No problem,' said the genie. 'Consider it granted, it's the least I can do. And as a special thank you, I will also guarantee you a long and healthy life so you can enjoy spending it!'

'And now for you, young lady, what can I grant you?' The genie asked.

With a broad smile on her face and a tone of excitement in her voice, she said. 'I'd like to own a celebrity style home in every country in the world, complete with servants.' She said.

'No problem, your wish is granted.' At that the genie snapped his fingers and said. 'For you, I will also grant that your homes will be safe from fire, burglary and any natural disasters!'

The couple hug and kiss each other at their success.

'Okay, now that we both have what we want,' the couple asked in unison, 'What is your wish genie?'

The genie sat back in his sofa, picked at his nails and said. 'Well, since I've been trapped in that bottle for more than a thousand years, and haven't been involved with a woman in all that time, my wish is to have passionate sex with your wife.

The husband turned to look at his wife and said, 'Well honey, you know we both have a fortune and all those houses because of him granting our wishes. What do you think?'

The wife mulled it over for a few moments and said, 'You know what darling, you're right. Considering our good fortune, I guess I wouldn't mind, but what about you, honey, are you okay with it?'

'You know I love you darling, with all my heart.' The husband said. 'So just know this . . . I'd do exactly the same for you!'

So the genie and the woman disappeared upstairs to the bedroom, where they spent the rest of the afternoon enjoying each other; the genie was insatiable.

After about three hours of non-stop erotic sex, the genie rolled over, lifted a packet of cigarettes from the bedside cabinet, took a cigarette out and lit up. Inhaling deeply, he blew the smoke out and looked directly into the woman's eyes and asked.

'How old are you and your husband?'

'We're both thirty-five years old.' She responded breathlessly.

'No kidding!' He said, drawing on his cigarette. 'Thirty-five years old and you both still believe in genies? Ha! Ha! Ha!'

Been There!

. . .

Most officers who have done their stint in plain-clothes duties will have experienced this sort of thing at least once during their time.

The entire shift enters the Mess room for briefing, with two of the shift allocated to work in plain-clothes.

During the tour of duty, the plain-clothes officers were detailed to attend a specific area and take up observations after several reports of vehicles being broken into. The officers concealed themselves in the shadows, one across the road in a garden and the other down a lane.

The first patrol car to venture into the area had the latest police recruit to the shift on board as passenger.

As he got out of the police car and started to walk towards a car, to check it, he saw a shadow of a person loitering in the lane, so he began to walk toward him . . . the same person, who only an hour or so previously, he had been talking to.

The plain-clothes officer, noticing it was his probationer uniformed colleague, turned and walked off, turning it into a gentle jog, then a sprint as he sped down the lane in a suspicious manner.

The young probationary constable ran after him, shouting, 'Stop, police! Stop, stop now!'

After about fifty or sixty metres, the plain-clothes officer stopped, turned around to face him and shouted, 'Surprise, surprise! Guess who?'

To which the young probationer replied with great gusto, 'Ya bastard!'

As his other colleagues appeared in the lane and burst out laughing.

Go For It

. . .

A friend of my missus was caught in a radar trap, exceeding the speed limit and was offered the option of attending a speed awareness course, as opposed to getting an endorsement on her driving licence.

She accepted the offer to attend.

On the day of her course, her daughter needed to use her car, therefore she opted to take the train. Unfortunately, the train was delayed and she arrived in the station late.

In an effort to make up time, she jumped into a taxi and called the training centre to make her excuses and offer an apology for missing the start of the course.

She was put through to the instructor's office, where she proceeded to reiterate her excuses for being late.

'Oh don't worry yourself about it, hen. Just tell your taxi driver to put his foot down and I'll see you when you get here!'

Not exactly what she expected to hear from the Speed Awareness Course.

Wedding Speech Tips

· · ·

There was a chief superintendent friend of mine who transferred up from West Midlands police several years ago.

He was marrying a much younger policewoman from his division and I was honoured to be asked to be his best man. So here's an excerpt of my speech.

They say it was love at first sight . . . A match made in heaven . . . They're like two peas in a pod . . . They're definitely made for each other. But they definitely weren't talking about these two. That was just some of the many comments friends, relatives and colleagues used to describe me and my wife at our wedding but we're not here today to talk about us. We're here to celebrate the coming together in marriage of Georgette and Tommy. Affectionately referred to by their best friends as G and T!

When Tommy told me that he and Georgette were going to be married. I have to admit, I was completely taken by surprise . . . More so that he'd only just found out himself. It was an open secret in police circles.

With the news of their impending marriage now officially public knowledge, there were a few things that had to be sorted out.

Tommy sat down with Georgette and asked her bluntly, if she was marrying him for love, or was it because he had a large commutation, police pension, several rented properties and various stocks and shares valued at approximately £1.5 to £2million pounds?

Georgette took great exception to this and said, 'Don't be so ridiculous Tommy Gunn . . . £2million! . . . Is that all your worth?'

Secondly, Tommy broached the subject with Georgette of how she felt about sex.

Georgette said that she would prefer if it was infrequently . . . Tommy sat back in his seat, took off his glasses, cleaned the lenses, put them back on and leaning forward he asked, 'When you say infrequently, was that one word or two?'

Tommy and I went out to celebrate their decision to get married, and I raised the subject about their age difference, there being twenty-six years of a difference, but Tommy just shrugged it off and said, 'Look Harry. If she dies, she dies!'

Afterwards, I called the waitress over and paid the bill. Tommy thanked me for doing so and said, he would have paid it himself, but his credit card had been stolen several weeks ago.

I asked if he had reported it to the police and he said very quietly, not yet, the thief spends less money than Georgette and her mother.

During the meal, Tommy was reminding me of how lucky he was to have met Georgette, having read an article in a magazine about how in some parts of Africa, a man doesn't know his wife at all, until he marries her. Sadly, I had to inform him, that it wasn't just in Africa, it happens here in Scotland as well!

I'll always remember the day that Georgette came into the police headquarters and asked Tommy to borrow his pride and joy MGB sports car, parked in the police car park.

Reluctantly, Tommy smiled and handed her the keys, but he was on tenterhooks as he paced up and down his office floor awaiting her return with it. The look on his face was priceless when she walked in the door and boldly announced, 'Tommy, you'll never guess who I've just bumped into?'

Fortunately for Tommy, when he regained consciousness Georgette explained she was in a shop at the time and not in his precious sports car.

Marriage is a wonderful, romantic thing and I say that from experience, as only last week, when I arrived home, I found my lovely wife sitting at the dining table looking over our marriage certificate! I asked her, 'What are you looking for darling?' To which she replied, 'An expiry date!'

She was joking, of course . . . I think!

And I can't help thinking about the wonderful honeymoon they have planned together and it reminded me of my own honeymoon. It was memorable in that we went off to Loch Ness and booked into a log cabin, what a wonderful experience. The very next morning I arose from our matrimonial bed, opened up the curtains and looked out at the bright sunshine as it reflected across the calm water of the loch. I turned to my new wife and said, 'It's a cracking day for the monster darling!'

To which she replied, 'If you bring that out again I'm going back to Glasgow!'

Finally, I'd like to take this opportunity to pass on some bits of advice I gave to Tommy.

Always remember this line, it could come in handy . . .
How do you expect me to remember your birthday darling, when you never look any older?

Finally, I must tell you about the time I was running the police office in Castlemilk, when a young bride of only five weeks called in, very upset. 'Officer,' she cried, 'My husband and I have just had a really dreadful fight! Things were thrown and terrible things were said.'

I told her to calm down that it was normal, every marriage has to have its first fight, but it's not half as bad as you think, so away back home and everything will be alright!

'No, I can't, too much has happened.' She said.

After a short while and a wee cup of tea, she relaxed and stopped crying. She then thanked me for my expert advice, and as she walked over to the door to leave, she paused for a moment, turned around and said, 'What do you think I should do with his body?'

Have a good life!

Bite Yer Lip!

...

While out on uniform patrol in the Castlemilk area, my partner observed the driver of the vehicle in front of us was not wearing his seatbelt.

Always on the lookout, we signalled the driver to pull over and stop and my colleague went to speak with the driver.

As it was, the driver was indeed not wearing his belt but immediately stated he had an exemption certificate from his doctor, indicating to the obvious fact that his right arm was amputated above the elbow.

The driver produced all his driving documents which were in order, after which I inspected his car for any obvious defects.

Two of the tyres fitted were passed their best and I suggested the matter would be best dealt with by issuing a vehicle defect rectification form (VDRS).

My partner was noting the details, while the driver waited patiently.

Seeing my partner struggle to tear off a copy of the VDRS form, I took it from him to pass to the driver. As I did so my colleague blurted out, 'I just don't have enough hands.'

Realising what he had just said, there was an awkward silence, thankfully broken by the driver who remarked. 'You can talk!'

Fortunately, the driver was able to laugh at himself and even showed us a tattoo he had done after his amputation surgery, which was a dotted line and a pair of scissors with the words, 'cut here', designed in the style of a form tear-off slip!

Now that was funny!

Mind you, he might have been 'armless, but he still got booked!

Spell Check!

· · ·

It never ceases to amaze me the amount of young police officers who have a problem with spelling ... it's unbelievable!

Such was the case when a young probationer constable submitted a report about an accused male and wrote, 'You were drunk and incapable in a public place and acting in a disorderly manor!'

Did he mean to write 'manner'?

Or was he in a 'manor', as in a rowdy household?

Answers in a stamped address envelope to me!

It's Snow Nice

. . .

In the 1980s, the Eaglesham Moor road, running from Eaglesham Village to the A77 Ayrshire, regularly had to be checked out during heavy snow falls because cars, vans and motorcyclists would end up stranded due to poor visibility, breaking down or more often than not, skidding off the roadway into a ditch!

On one particular occasion I was on patrol in a Range Rover. Due to snowy weather conditions I received instructions, along with big Kenny Morrison, to perform a snow patrol check along the moor road because of the adverse weather conditions, with a view to it being closed off to all vehicular traffic.

Force Control were on the radio every few minutes looking for 'an update on the weather and road conditions on the moor'.

In the bleak darkness and totally blizzard conditions, we stopped several times due to the poor visibility. Big Kenny had to get out and check the road in front of us, while I drove and each time he got back into the Range Rover he was even more freezing and covered from head to foot in snow than before. We decided it was better to stop and wait patiently until it cleared before venturing any further.

Suddenly, something came skittling down the road, hit the side of the Range Rover on the passenger side and carried on.

At the very same moment, force control came back on the radio requesting an update on the weather conditions.

Now big Kenny Morrison, having just had a fright, was not the most subtle or patient of cops and was renowned for having a short fuse. This coupled with the fact he had been in and out of the vehicle several times, in atrocious conditions (and each time he got back in, I would sing the theme from the *Snowman*, 'We're walking in the air . . .') it was obvious that he'd had enough of the snow, me and Force Control.

He snapped! He grabbed the police radio, wrenching it from the dashboard and blurted out aggressively.

'Tango Mike Fourteen to Force Control. Would you please note it's fecken snowing so fecken heavy here I can't see the fecken front of the Range Rover. I've been in and out more times than a fecken Swiss cukoo in a clock and you're on the fecken radio every two fecken minutes pestering me for a fecken snow update! Well, Here it is, it's fecken snowing . . . Alright?'

There was a pause of several moments silence, then the controller replied rather hesitantly, 'Roger Tango Mike Fourteen, I take it from that response, it's bad!'

Won't Get Fooled Again!

• • •

In 1980, Jimmy Boyler, a notorious Glasgow gangster was released from the Barlinnie Special Unit on appeal after being convicted of a double contract murder and sentenced to life imprisonment, with the recommendation he serve a minimum twenty-five year jail sentence.

He immediately arranged a 'get away from it all holiday' in Africa after his release from prison to avoid the media.

While on a hike through the African bush, he stumbled across a young bull elephant standing with one leg raised in the air.

The elephant seemed to be distressed, so Jimmy (being an animal lover, if not a humanist) approached it with great caution.

He got down on one knee, inspected the distressed elephant's foot, and found a large piece of wood deeply embedded in it.

Being a recognised expert with a blade, Jimmy took out his trusty flick knife and as carefully and gently as he could, he worked the wood out, after which the elephant gingerly put down its foot.

The elephant then turned to Jimmy, and with a rather curious look in its eyes, stared at him for several tense moments.

Jimmy stood frozen to the spot, thinking of nothing else but being trampled by this enormous, ungrateful animal.

However, totally the opposite occurred, as the elephant trumpeted loudly, turned and walked away in the other direction with a new 'sense of freedom'.

Jimmy would never forget that terrifying incident, or the events of that day.

Eighteen years later, Jimmy was considered to be a reputable and highly regarded artist with a young wife and family. On this particular day, he was walking through the Calderpark Zoo along with his young family eating candy-floss and ice cream.

As they approached the elephant enclosure, one of the creatures turned and walked over to where Jimmy and his young family were standing looking on. It was a large bull elephant. It stopped and stared at Jimmy then suddenly; it lifted its front foot off the ground and slammed it down.

The elephant did that several times before trumpeting loudly.

All the while staring intently at Jimmy.

Remembering his own encounter with a young bull elephant in 1980, Jimmy couldn't help wondering, if this was the same one that he had helped all these years ago ... So Jimmy, wanting to impress his young wife and family, summoned up the courage to climb over the metal railing and enter the enclosure.

He slowly and cautiously walked right up to the elephant and looked straight into its eyes.

The elephant looked at him with a 'sense of freedom' and great excitement in its eyes it trumpeted again, Jimmy smiled ecstatically, as it rubbed its trunk against his face and as he turned to smile at his family, and pose for the obligatory family photo, the elephant wrapped its broad, affectionate trunk around one of Jimmy's legs ...

And promptly slammed him against the wall and railing, killing him instantly.

It probably wasn't the same elephant, but then again, who really gives a TOSS. It was a nice wee story, I thought!

And Justice was served after all!!

Is That Right?

• • •

Sunday morning sermon will be about: 'Jesus Walking on the Water'.

Sunday evening sermon will be focussed on: 'Searching for Jesus'.

Court Jesters

. . .

It's official . . . the Scottish Justice system has become a complete and utter joke; a benevolent institution openly promoting the welfare of criminals.

Well what's new really? It's been going that way for several years with Sheriffs and Judges too old and out of date with what is happening on our streets.

It's a complete reversal with some of them, the criminals are the victims and the victims and the police witnesses are the accused villains.

One of the latest incidents that I have read is so perverse and ridiculous; you just couldn't make it up. It involves a sheriff lifting an imposed curfew of a violent criminal, who openly admitted to breaking the legal restriction and committing a series of crimes, including assault and housebreaking, whilst serving a previously imposed curfew.

The sheriff, in his wisdom, (bloody idiot) decided that, by lifting the ned's curfew, 'it would help him to socialise, meet up with and make new friends,' or other neds like himself.

Friends my arse! It's a licence to commit more crimes.

Call me slightly cautious and perhaps a tad suspicious but in my mind, it's more likely he is looking out for new, 'unsuspecting, law abiding, decent living punters to terrorise and physically assault, oh and more houses to break into while the owners are out trying to earn a living doing real work in the community!'

Well why not? The sheriff has just handed him a licence to do this, while awaiting sentence for previous crimes of which he was found guilty and isn't it great to know that in doing so, he has totally ignored every decent, law abiding member of the public.

This is the same wee ned, who prior to this show of leniency, was given permission by the courts to fly off for a week's holiday to Spain.

All the while his latest victim recovered in hospital from the injuries sustained when assaulted by him!

It must be extremely reassuring to everyone out there that a convicted, violent criminal and persistent offender is being allowed to walk the streets of our neighbourhood every night to socialise.

No wonder so many of my former colleagues and members of the public are sickened with the sentencing by some of our so-called sheriffs and have to constantly remind themselves why they bother to catch the 'bad' guys. The words ned, criminal, thug and accused, appear to translate into, Victim! Victim! Victim! And Victim!

The Big Yin

· · ·

Two Glesca mates were out for a drink and after several pints they both rush off to the toilet. As they stood there, Tam peered over and noticed that his mate Charlie was very well endowed and asked him what was the secret of having a big 'boaby'!

Charlie owned up and told him that he didn't always have a big 'boaby', but he'd visited a cosmetic surgeon who said, for £6,000, he could perform a small operation and make him more of a man. Tam was so impressed he asked Charlie for the name of the surgeon and contacted him to arrange a private consultation.

A few months later, they both met up again in the pub toilet, whereupon Charlie asked Tam if he had contacted the surgeon? 'Take a gander for yourself mate.' Tam said. 'Whit dae ye think of that beast? And it only cost me a third of the money that you paid for yours.'

Charlie, meanwhile had a right good look, then said, 'Nae offence Tam, but ye've been bumped! Nae wunner it was a third o' the price o' mine. The fly bugger's only gone and gave ye my auld yin'!

Facebook Liar

...

My old colleague Donnie Henderson, opened up a Facebook account, thinking he would network, meet new friends, sound very interesting to some unsuspecting lonely females and hopefully find a partner of the opposite sex for friendship and maybe romance.

He was asked by a female to be friends and he agreed to her request, even though her profile picture was that of a labrador puppy! Mind you her personal description was very impressive: professional woman, forty-ish, quite flirty, athletic, good looking, emotionally settled, good debater, open minded, carefree, outgoing, passionate, voluptuous, loves walks in the country, seeking a soul mate.

With those personal details, it is no wonder Donnie was smitten and communicated with her almost every hour of the day. This continued for several weeks and it was only a matter of time before they set up a date to meet.

The big day arrived and the meeting place set. Donnie arrived early, armed with flowers and smelling like a dish of potpourri . . . Yuck!

Suddenly, she appeared from out of nowhere, and I really mean that. Poor Donnie didn't even recognise her. The only thing resembling her description was the Glasgow *Herald* she was carrying in her left hand.

Unlike Donnie, an ex-polis, who told the truth about himself and uploaded a recent, albeit ten years old, photograph of himself in police uniform, his Facebook date was the exact opposite and lied through her teeth, those that she still had left in her mouth.

Donnie was gagging for it and went along with the game, putting on a brave face.

However, if she had put up a true description, it would have read like this . . .

'Forty-nine year old bitch with no tits, ugly, needing a shave due to heavy medication and body hair growing out of everywhere, very argumentative but gagging for it, loves a good swally in the house or in the pub, followed by a face sucking session, sleeps in a tent with other campers, and is basically looking for a randy old stalker with a few bob!'

They said it would never last . . . and it didn't.

After she had devoured her third Super Size Big Mac Meal with extra fries, she excused herself to pay a visit to the ladies loo or as she so politely put it, 'Keep an eye on my chips big man, I'm taking time out for a dump!'

During this unforseen break in the romantic proceedings, big Donnie took advantage of the situation to promptly do a runner! Upon returning home to the safety of his wee hoose, he deleted her contact details and duly pulled the plug on his Facebook account!

However, for all you lonely hearts out there, here are Harry's Agony Aunt safety survival tips to all men.

Recent studies have found that women find various male faces attractive, depending on where they are in their menstrual cycle.

It has also been noted that when a woman is ovulating, she prefers a man with rugged masculine features. It has not gone unnoticed that George Michael, Boy George and John Barrowman have intimated they share the same preference!

However, a word of caution!

One must be extremely careful when a woman is menstruating. This is the moment when she prefers her man soaked in petrol and duly set on fire with the added extras of pins and needles stuck in both eyes and an openly extended golfing umberella shoved up his arse to the handle!

In other words, not exactly a good time for the male species to get involved sexually!

Whit's He Oan Aboot?
• • •
David Cameron has announced that he intends to make it more difficult to claim benefits, so from next week all the forms will be printed in English. 'D'ye fink he's gettin' at aw us Gleswegians, or whit?'

My Pal Charles

. . .

When I worked in the Crime Intelligence (CID), I was privileged to obtain, through my friend Duncan, the telephone number for Buckingham Palace. No big deal really, but I used it to my advantage one night during a police night out with some Special Branch officers and other CID departmental cops, when we were all meeting up and drinking in a well known establishment.

During the evening we were all getting a bit tipsy (pissed!) and there was one particular Special Branch cop who was a bit loose with his mouth and exaggerating about an assignment he had been on involving some of the young Royals.

I couldn't resist it. It would be like putting his gas at a peep, big time!

'Funny you should say that, I was just talking to Prince Charles the other day!' I then said nothing else, but there was a very noticeable silence for a few moments, before the Special Branch officer said.

'Aye right! You don't know Prince Charles. You're at the wind up Harry!'

'Don't think so, son. I have called him a few times recently for a chat!'

Several of them laughed, then, they one by one stuttered to a stop.

'So you've got Prince Charles personal telephone number?'

'Well how else could I have called him! And why wouldn't I have it? We're friends. I've escorted him and

Diana on numerous visits.' I replied, nonchalantly and convincingly. 'Don't you believe me?' I said.

At this point, he looked around at several of the other officers sitting around us and said, 'Yeah right. Well let's just give him a call then!'

To which I responded immediately with, 'Okay! But I'll call him, since you don't believe me and you can ask him, personally, if he knows me and how we met.'

At that, I called the number on my mobile and handed it to him to listen.

After a few rings, the phone was answered and the male voice said, 'Buckingham Palace, can I help you?'

He was so surprised by the voice on the phone answering 'Buckingham Palace', he immediately, hung up and handed me the phone.

Since that day, he has never questioned me again, and I must admit, I regularly took advantage of my position, as Prince Charles' friend!

Cheers Duncan!

Wee Fishes

...

I was out with my wife Marion and our friend Sonia from All Talents UK, with her date Jason, who has a business with fish. He charges people for the privilege of putting their bare feet into the tanks of fish and having them eat all their dead skin from between their toes and whatever else they might fancy. Not exactly my idea of a pedicure, but apparently very popular with the locals.

'It's also very relaxing for them!' He added.

So I had an idea between drinks.

'Jason! I have a business proposition for you. While your punters are being pleasured by your feet-eating fish, so to speak, and, as you say, are totally relaxing while paying for the pleasure. Why don't I supply you with some of my *Harry the Polis* books, so they can have a laugh at the same time?' It was just a business idea!

PS, He also received a phone call during our drinking session, informing him that one of his shops had discovered about thirty of his prized 'munchers' dead!

Always thinking, with money making ideas in my head, I immediately suggested, he sell them to the local sushi bar.

Not that I eat there, but who's going to know when it's mixed in amongst a few bits of rice!!

Gentleman Ned

...

My very good friend Eliot was relating a story to me that occurred many years ago in the Knightsbridge area of London. Very posh!

He had just been for dinner with his girlfriend and had returned to his car, parked a short distance from the restaurant.

He was getting ready to start the engine, when his girlfriend said, 'There's a man walking down the line of cars behind us scoring all their paintwork with a metal object.'

Eliot looked into his rear view mirror and saw the figure of a man.

The male suspect continued with the same malicious act as he scratched the paintwork of Eliot's car while he was present inside it, sitting in front of his steering wheel looking out.

The suspect walked along the cars parked in the line in front, before disappearing round a corner and out of sight.

Eliot informed his female passenger to remain in the car while he went after the male responsible.

As he ran round the corner, he saw a very tall male casually walking along the road. Unsure if this was the person responsible but with no one else in sight, he went up to him and said, 'Excuse me, but did you just scratch the paintwork on my car with a metal object?'

'I'm not sure, so you tell me!' He replied.

'Well, I think it was you and the object that you used is in your pocket, so empty your pockets now. Come on, quickly. Let's see what you have in your pocket.' Eliot said with a voice of authority.

The suspect responded immediately by putting his hand into his pocket and pulling out a bunch of house keys.

'Keys! That's what you used,' said Eliot, convinced he had got his man. 'Right, now I would appreciate it, if you would accompany me to the police station'.

'By all means!' Said the suspect. 'Lead the way.'

At that, Eliot walked off, closely followed by his tall suspect.

After about 100 metres, Eliot stopped, looked at his accompanying suspect and asked, 'You wouldn't happen to know where the local police office is?'

The suspect said he did and as a result, they performed a role reversal, with the tall suspect walking off in the direction of the police office, closely followed by the mild mannered Eliot.

Moments later, on arriving at the front door of the police office, the suspect stopped, and showing impeccable manners, as he turned to Eliot and said, 'After you, old boy!'

Eliot entered, went up to the front desk and reported to the office sergeant, 'This man just scratched the bodywork of my car and several others parked nearby.'

The police sergeant asked Eliot if he saw him doing it and Eliot replied, 'No, but I followed the person round the corner and he was the only person in the street and the keys that he used to do it are in his trouser pocket.'

'That's all very well.' Said the sergeant, 'but did you see him do it?'

Eliot paused for a moment, 'No! But my girlfriend saw him. She's in the car. Wait here and I'll go and get her.'

At that, Eliot ran along the road to his car and, moments later, returned at the office with his girlfriend.

As it was, she only saw him from behind but was convinced this was the same person who damaged Eliot's car and identified him as the suspect.

Having listened to his account of what had occurred, the desk sergeant turned to the suspect and asked him straight out, 'Did you scratch his car with your keys?'

'I most certainly did.' He responded immediately without any thought, adding. 'And I'd like several others to be taken into account as well.'

Eliot and the desk sergeant were shocked and surprised at the open admission of guilt by the suspect.

The suspect was charged with the damage to all the vehicles involved.

However, looking back on it now, Eliot still gets the shivers when he thinks about it and finds it hard to believe he acted in the way he did with a suspect almost a foot taller than him in height and built like a 'brick shithouse' but, as it was, it worked out on this occasion.

And believe me, you couldn't make this scenario up.

Mind you, thirty years on, older and much wiser, I've convinced Eliot not to ever attempt the same stunt in Glasgow. Somehow, I don't think the local Glesca ned would be so accommodating in showing the same courteous manners that this English gentleman afforded him.

Forget the Change

. . .

A Jewish woman telephones her mother and says, 'Mum! I'm divorcing Joshua! All he ever wants is sex, sex, sex! My vagina is now the size of a fifty pence piece . . . It used to be the size of a five pence piece.'

Her mother says, 'You're married to a multi-millionaire businessman, you live in a sixteen bedroom mansion in Bearsden, you're driving a top of the range, Ferrari sports car. Not only that, you get £2,000 a week spending allowance and you have four holidays abroad each year and you want to throw all that away for a measly forty-five pence?'

There was silence on the phone for a moment, then the daughter said, 'Have to go Mum, I feel a holiday in Las Vegas coming on!'

He No' Be Back!

...

My old colleague Peter Connoby was on his days off when there was a knock at his front door.

He opened it, to see Detective John Frame standing there.

'Ah need ye tae come wi' me, Peter. I've an enquiry at the local paper shop managed by Asians along the road and require a witness!'

'So whit's the enquiry?' Peter asked him.

'Och, a big Asian boy was stopped a few weeks ago by the traffic cops wi' a van load of cigarettes, tobacco and cigars and didnae have any receipts for proof of purchase for the van load of tobacco in the back, so they confiscated them, while they made enquiries. Subsequently, I was given the enquiry tae dae but the fiscal has since said I have to return them tae him! So that's whit we're dayin.'

Peter quickly dressed and off they went in the unmarked police van to the shop.

On arrival outside, Peter said, 'Do you want me to start humphin' the boxes of fags in?'

'Naw, no' yet Peter.' Said John. 'Let's have a wee word wi' him first.' At that, they both entered the shop.

Once inside, they went straight to the counter and identified themselves as police officers to the shopkeeper.

'We're looking for Anwar Butt, is he here?' Asked John with authority.

'I'm afraid not sir, he's gone.' Replied the shopkeeper.

'Where's he gone?'

'He's gone home sir ... Won't be back.' Said the shopkeeper.

'Well, when will he be back? I need tae see him.' John said.

'No' be back. He's gone home to Pakistan . . . Never coming back!'

'Never?' Replied John.

'Never again!' He said, as a matter of fact.

'Never, ever coming back again?' John asked once more.

'Yes sir! Never ever coming back again, ever!' He added.

'Aw well. Ah suppose that's it then.' Said John. 'We might as well go Peter. There's nuthin' we can do now.'

At that, they started to walk to the door, when the shop-keeper shouted after them, 'Please sir, what did he do?'

John nonchalantly turned around to face him and replied, 'He never done anything . . . I've got a few thousand fags and tobacco in the van belonging tae him and was just wanting tae gie him them back, but if he's not coming back, there's no' a lot I can do.'

Quick as a flash, the shopkeeper said, 'You can give them to me, I'll take them for him.'

'I'd love tae gie ye them, pal,' John replied, 'but I can only return them tae the complainer himself and as you've just stated, he's "never ever coming back again, ever" to this country, so we'll just have tae make arrangements tae dispose of them. But thanks for the offer.'

At that, they left the shop and drove off.

Later that week, the confiscated haul of unclaimed cigarettes, cigars and tobacco were disposed off, as per the Bishopbriggs police procedure manual . . .

Efficiently and cordially administered by Detective Constable John Frame.

And as a result, the entire Bishopbriggs office was reeking like an auld lum for several weeks afterwards.

Fortunately, the Fire Station was right next door!

Grim Reaper
...

Donnie called me last night to say he dreamt that The Grim Reaper came for him and he had to beat him off with the vacuum cleaner.

'Fuxsakes, Harry, talk about Dyson with death!'

I Hear You Knocking
...

The next door neighbour started banging on my door at 2.30am this morning, can you believe that 2.30am?

Fortunately for him I was still up playing my bagpipes!

Harry's Joke Pages

. . .

Ah think that wife of mine is trying to give me a heart attack. The other night she came in from the bingo and announced, 'Ye're never gonnae believe this!'

'Ye've won the jackpot darling!' I blurted out with excitement.

She shook her head and replied, 'No! I'm pregnant . . .

'All I could hear as I lost consciousness was her saying 'I'm only kidding ya dafty!'

I got my own back when she was standing looking into the mirror, rubbing her eyes and making wide movements with her mouth.

'I wonder how I could get rid of all these wrinkles from my face?' she said.

'Loosen your bra.' I suggested.

Not exactly the best response I could have given, but it was spontaneous.

Went into my local pub the other night and ordered up a pint of Bellhaven beer.

As Jim the barman put it down, he said, 'Watch yer pint Harry. A few of the boys in the darts team turned their backs the other night and some bugger drank them.

With this in mind, I later had to go to the toilet, so I took out my pen and wrote on the beer mat, 'I've just spat in this!' and sat it on top of my pint.

When I returned, some bugger had written underneath, 'So have I!'

I've just put a deposit down on a brand new Porsche and mentioned on Facebook, 'I can't wait for the new 911 to arrive!'

Next thing I know 4,000 Muslims have added me as a friend!

My wife wanted an iPad for Christmas. So I got her the next best thing, an Eye Patch . . . Pure quality man!

I was passing over the KGV Bridge the other morning when I saw George Galloway fall into the River Clyde.

As a responsible citizen I immediately contacted the emergency services. They still haven't responded and I'm starting to think I've wasted a stamp.

I nearly won the Lottery the other night there, I was only six numbers away.

Ian Paisley has been diagnosed with Alzheimer's, bless him. He was seen last week walking around the streets of Belfast shouting 'No Remember!'

Pub Quiz in Glasgow, and it's the final question for the jackpot of £1,000. 'The question is about pop music. Now for £1,000 Take That's first CD album consisted of four words, the first two were Take That, but what were the other two?'

There was total silence in the pub. You could hear a pin drop. Then a wee Glesca man shouted out, 'I've got it. Wis it, "Ya Bastard"?'

I was driving this morning when I saw an AA recovery van parked up.

The driver was sobbing uncontrollably and looked very miserable. I thought to myself, 'That guy's heading for a breakdown.'

I was recently reading up on Scotland's greatest bard, Robert Burns. I couldn't believe it when I read about what he achieved in a very short thirty-seven year lifespan. Not only as a world renowned poet, composer of some of the world's most romantic love songs, a tax collector, a hard working farmer but also as an amazing lover . . .

I mention that only because he had approximately thirteen children to five different women, as well as two sets of twins and a few others to his long suffering Jean . . . As we say in Glasgow . . .

'What a shagger!'

Ebay
...

Big Donnie was just telling me he spent £40 on ebay last week, bidding for a penis enlarger.

He said, 'I've just opened up the parcel and the bastard has sent me a frigging magnifying glass!'

Police Desk

...

During the 1970s and '80s there was a police programme on Scottish Television called *Police Desk* introduced by the author and TV presenter Bill Knox, seeking information from viewers to help solve particular crimes.

It became very popular and as a result, the TV producers decided to give it a spectacular introduction.

As it was, they wanted to start with a police Range Rover, headlights, blue lights and sirens blaring, being filmed speeding along the Clydeside Expressway and onto the flyover leading to the Kingston Bridge with all the traffic moving out of their way, allowing them to pass.

It was an impressive start to the programme, but little did the public know, that the start wasn't exactly filmed at the first take. What happened was, my colleagues Ian Thomson and Alex Sterrick were in the Range Rover recording the 'emergency' start. They were being filmed leaving the expressway to go onto the flyover, when an elderly woman driver looked into her rear view mirror, saw the police coming up fast and instead of moving over, she panicked and slammed on her brakes!

Due to this unrehearsed and unexpected manoeuvre by the lady driver, Ian had to take evasive action to avoid colliding with her.

He braked . . .

He swerved . . .

He lost control!

And promptly . . . Crashed into the metal barrier! . . .

CUT!

Tyred Of Neds

. . .

One sunny afternoon at Cambuslang big Richard and Davy, the local beat men, were finishing their shift duty when one of the local neds and his sidekick drove around the rear of the police office in his shiny new sports car and parked up.

It was obvious that he was over the moon with his new car but was somewhat annoyed that after only two days of owning it, he had been stopped and issued with a ticket and a form to produce his driving licence and insurance at the police office.

Feeling a wind up in the air Davy complimented him on his new, smart looking sports car but pointed out that his tyre valves were not in alignment properly with his wheels.

'Are they meant tae be exactly the same?' asked the ned.

'Oh aye, especially a new, expensive car like yours! I'm totally shocked at that.' said Davy.

'So how will I sort that then?'

'Well, if you jack up your car, you can position the wheels so that all of the valves are at the top, in the same position. Makes it run smoother.'

So, the ned and his sidekick promptly opened the boot of his car and started jacking it up and removing each wheel as he went around his car, lining the valves up at the top.

Afterwards, sweating profusiouly and out of breath with their effort, Davy advised him to keep an eye on them in case they went out again because some traffic cops would book you for it.

Later that same week Richard and Davy heard from the owner of the local garage, that the ned had called in regarding wheel alignment, saying that he was warned by two big polis that he could be charged if they were not aligned exactly the same.

'Did you charged him for doing it?' asked Davy.

'Of course I charged him! I took £6 a wheel.' said the garage owner.

'Good! He'll probably notice they'll go out of alignment on a weekly basis. So here's hoping he has plenty of money . . . and time!' Ha! Ha!

Some neds believe everything you tell them and waste money for fun!

Tip Off
. . .

One day a young ned from Govanhill called me at the Gorbals police office and said, 'I just saw a poor old woman fall over on the ice today, right outside the chippie!

At least I think she was poor. She only had £1.20 in her purse'.

Say What You Mean

. . .

Which reminds me of another wee police automobile story.

It happened one day when the crew of Lima Delta Four were out on uniform mobile patrol duty and they punctured a tyre.

As the crew members got out to change it with the spare wheel they soon discovered that the wheel brace spanner they had was from another police vehicle and didn't fit their particular car.

So they called up the control room and explained the situation, informing them that they needed assistance at their locus.

The female controller instinctively broadcast the following message; 'Lima Delta control to Lima Delta Six. Could you please rendevouz with Lima Delta Four at his location and assist him with your tool, as his tool is too small and doesn't fit and he thinks you have a much bigger one . . .'

'Oh my God . . . I can't believe I just broadcast that!'

Aragosa!

...

During our trip to America recently, we drove down the West coast. Las Vegas, Mammoth Lakes, Death Valley, San Francisco. But one of the strangest, weirdest places we visited was Aragosa, a very small town on our way to Death Valley.

We noticed some women sitting on rocking chairs outside on the wooden porch of the Aragosa Motel and pulled up alongside to ask them directions.

One of them immediately jumped to her feet and welcomed us to Aragosa, while the other two remained seated, greeting us with their toothless smiles. In hindsight, they resembled the postcard photos we saw of Death Valley!

It was also noticeable that Aragosa lacked a dentist or a shop selling toothpaste, as all three portrayed missing teeth at the front of their mouths and more noticeably, they all weighed in excess of twenty stones . . . Easy!

The town possibly had a bigger population but these three ate them all.

'Is this a town?' I asked.

'Yup, sure is honey. Would ya like ta stay and check in? We have vacancies. We'll let ya pick yar own room!'

At this point my wife is nipping my arm because any minute now she's expecting a Norman Bates look a like to come running out from behind the motel desk wearing a granny wig, Paisley pattern apron and wielding a very large butcher's knife, with music playing in the background. 'Ching! – Ching! – Ching! – Ching!'

She continued talking, 'We have seven inhabitants, a motel, an opera house and a bar diner on the corner there, honey. We used ta have a store and gas station but it closed up several years ago.'

Inhabitants: seven! Repeat, seven!

Yes folks, it's not a typing error, I do mean seven in total. The three on the forecourt, were carers for the elderly owner of the town, who apparently bought it about thirty years ago and was now bedridden.

I was totally gob-smacked but couldn't resist taking it further, much to the annoyance of my wife.

'Have you any guests in the motel just now?'

'Not at the moment honey but we might have soon.' She replied.

'Seven inhabitants you say! Well you've accounted for four, where are the others?' (Have you really eaten them? I thought!)

'Well, Dan and Teri run the bar diner, and Teri junior does all the odd jobs in the town . . . fixing this 'n' that.' She said. 'The special today is Teri's corned beef and cabbage with biscuits 'n' gravy. It's yummy!'

'Well, we might just visit Dan and Teri's and sample it . . . Thanks!' At that, with Marion's nails sunk deep into my skin and drawing blood, I drove over to the diner for a look.

We parked the car and went inside. I couldn't come all this way to America and discover a place like Aragosa without checking it all out.

As we entered the diner, we were met by Teri . . . or was it Dan! Take your pick, but she was humongous! And he, Dan . . . or Teri was the chef.

We sat at a table and she . . . Well let's just refer to her as 'Godzilla', presented us with a menu, pointing out the 'Daily Special', corned beef and cabbage. After a few moments, we decided to take the safe option of chicken with courgettes and French fries. They can't do too much damage there! We thought.

We sat at opposite sides of the table, Marion watching my back and me watching her's (Music) 'Ching! – Ching! – Ching! – Ching! – Ching!'

'Sorry darling but I have to go to the toilet.' I announced.

'Do you have to go now?' She asked.

'Well if I don't, she'll probably rub my nose in it, darling!'

'Make it quick.' She replied like a ventriloquist, without moving her lips.

As I passed the kitchen entrance en route to the toilet, I could see her cutting through pieces of chicken with what appeared like garden secateurs. Snip! Snip! Snip!

After a few moments, I returned to my table.

'What was that clicking noise?' My wife asked.

'What clicking noise?' I replied, teasing her.

'I could hear a loud clicking noise, coming from the kitchen.' She said.

'Oh, was it . . . "Snip! Snip! Snip!"?' I asked.

'Aye, that was it!' She responded, eager to hear my reply.

'It was just Godzilla, she was sitting on the edge of the sink, clipping her toe nails.'

She looked at me in disbelief and I knew there and then I had taken it toooooo far.

'Only kidding darling, I'm only kidding . . . Sit down.' I pleaded, as she was heading for the exit.

After a few moments of grovelling on my part to calm her down, Godzilla appeared from the back-shop carrying our meals and placed them on the table in front of us.

'Can I get you anything else?' She asked, reluctantly.

Looking down at my plate, I had to resist asking her if she had killed the chicken humanely or had it just drowned in the excess oil on my plate!

I reckon I had enough oil to service a family car.

Marion looked at her plate . . . Looked at me . . . And said, 'Pay the bill, I'll wait for you in the car. Don't take too long or you'll be checking in with "Baby Jane" and her two sisters over at Bates Motel.'

That said, she made a hasty exit from the diner, followed moments later by yours truly . . .

Minus $40 for the pleasure!

Well! You have to tip accordingly for good service and there's no way I was going to wait about for change and upset her any more.

After the experience of Aragosa, Death Valley was a dawdle!

Nurse Munro

...

My sister Kim was relating a story about Linda Munro, a fellow student nurse she enrolled with when training.

While working in the Western Infirmary, in Glasgow, Linda was told to go to the waiting room and assist an elderly gentleman out-patient and take him to the toilet. He'd suffered a stroke and had restricted use of his hands.

Nervous at the prospect, she entered the packed waiting room and was confronted with several grey haired men.

She moved nervously and slowly through the room from chair to chair saying the patient's name, hoping someone would respond and acknowledge her.

Eventually, one man got up out of his seat as she approached him, so she politely took hold of his hand and asked him to follow her to the toilets.

Totally embarrassed and unable to look the patient in the face, she closed the cubicle door behind him and began to fondle with his trousers.

After a few moments, the elderly patient took hold of her hands and said, 'I'm dreadfully sorry my dear, as much as I would love you to continue, I'm only here to visit my father.'

Don't you just love it being a BUPA patient!

Eye, Right!

· · ·

A wee Govan mercenary soldier walked into his local bar and the barman said, 'How's it gaun wee man, long time no see. Whit's the Hampden roar (score) wi' ye? Ye're looking a wee bit Alan Rough.'

'Whit dae ye mean?' asked the wee mercenary, 'I'm feeling tickety boo.'

'Whit's up wi' yer John Greig (leg) then? Ye didnae have that before.'

'Aw ye noticed!' said the mercenary, 'We were in a fight one day wi' some o' that Taliban mob and I copped a hit wi' a grenade, but I've got an artificial one on, so am tickety boo.'

The barman replied, 'Okay, I can see that but whit about that dodgy looking Charlie Cook (hook)? Where's yer haun?'

The mercenary explained, 'Well, that happened in another fight when we boarded a Somalia kidnappers' boat during a rescue mission and got attacked by a big bastard wi' a machete. Cut my frigging haun off.

'Fortunately the medic that wis way us fitted me oot wi' a hook but I'm tickety boo. Really!'

'Whit about yer ol' Dave MacKay (eye)? Whit's that aw aboot then? Wearing a Tony Hatch (patch)?'

'Oh this?' the wee mercenary said, pointing to his eye. 'That wis just a wee accident that happened when a wis coming o'er on the Renfrew Ferry and a flock o' burds flew o'er.

'Ah looked up, and one o' them shat right in my eye.'

'Ye're joking!' Said the bartender. 'Ye didnae lose an eye cause a burd shat in it did ye?'

'Aye! . . . It wis early days and ah wis still trying tae get used tae my hook!'

Love Again
. . .

A wee Glesca ned had a pre-arranged meeting to see his ex-wife after many years of living apart during a drawn out divorce.

It would be an understatement to say he was pleasantly taken by complete surprise with how much she had changed in her appearance. She had lost weight, slimmed down and now had a figure hugging shape, her hair was professionally cut like Meg Ryan's and now dyed blonde; she looked absolutely stunning.

He couldn't resist her new look and instantly fell in love with her all over again and decided well, while we're both here, why not make love once more for old time's sake!

He couldn't believe how good the sex was between them after all these years, they were gelling perfectly, without an angry word being spoken, when he was suddenly interrupted by two police officers who entered the room and showed their utter disgust at was taking place, after all, he was only there to identify her body.

Who Am I?

· · ·

One Monday morning the local community policeman was walking through his neighbourhood beat area, on his usual route, to the local school.

On his way past some of the more plush bungalows, he noticed that one in particular had several cars parked in the driveway.

He was about to pass by, when Denis, the householder, came out the front door carrying a large bin bag of empty beer, wine, and spirit bottles for the recycling bin.

'Gee wiz Denis, looks like you had one hell of a party last night.' The community cop remarked.

Denis looked up and replied, 'Actually, we had a bit of a bash on Saturday night and this is the first I have felt like moving since Sunday morning. We had about twelve couples from around the neighbourhood over for some weekend fun and it got a bit wild and over the top. We all got so drunk that around midnight, we started playing a game of, 'WHO AM I?'

The community cop, paused for a moment then asked, 'So how do you play WHO AM I?'

'Well, all the men go into the bedroom and come out one at a time covered with a bed sheet with their 'family jewels' sticking out through a hole in the sheet. Then the female partners have to try and guess who it is underneath.'

The community cop laughed and said, 'Sounds like a real fun party, I wish I'd been there.'

To which Denis replied, 'Probably a good thing you weren't. Your name came up five times.'

The Earth Moved

. . .

As we all know, many people in our society have different sexual preferences, from the missionary position to the . . . non-missionary position. Not being very sexually adventurous myself, I won't go into this in too much detail!

The thing is though, we don't always see it in other people and they don't always talk about such a delicate, personal subject in open conversation, unless they've had a few pints of beer first.

However, a situation arose recently with Stella, an ex-policewoman friend and colleague of mine while relaxing with a drink at a police reunion. Totally out of the blue, she confided in me and spilled the beans, so to speak, by relating a scenario regarding a recent relationship she had with a man she met while surfing the internet!

As it was, she just happened to come across a dating webiste that claimed it would find her a match based on the private details of her relationship status, hobbies and, most importantly when networking for memebers of the opposite sex, her own sexual preferences. Being a 'single white female', she decided to investigate it further, by enrolling and submitting her details.

Like the feeling of excitement when winning the proverbial jackpot of a 'one armed bandit' in a Las Vegas casino, her number came up and she was matched with Justin.

Justin's profile had similar likes and dislikes, in politics, music, eating habits, but added his 'love' for romance and sexual ecstasy with the right person. As an added bonus, he was slightly older, with several successful businesses in his portfolio making him a potential 'Sugar Daddy!' . . . Kerr-chingg!

After exchanging the pleasantries with each other, they found enough similarities to arrange their first date, through in the neutral city of Edinburgh.

Off Stella went to the Chic hair salon to see Gillian and have her roots dyed. Then to the nail bar for Wendy to apply some long, manicured false nails and finally, she finished off with the ultimate special offer in spray-on tan from Susan, all designed to impress on her romantic weekend date with her computer generated opposite sex 'match'.

The day of their meeting arrived and surprise, surprise, he actually matched his profile picture but there was obviously a dyslexic typing error with his height, having submitted it as 6'3" but in real life, with his 'club' boots on and standing on his tippytoes, he barely registered 5'3". However, Stella decided that you have to take the good with the bad and his height wasn't an issue, particularly when you're both lying down.

After the initial introduction, they went out on a 'short' sightseeing tour of auld reekie, (sorry about the 'short pun'), before returning to their hotel room for a kiss and cuddle, before getting changed into something more glamorous for her romantic meal in the plush hotel restaurant.

As she entered the dining room, looking quite stunning in her dress, Justin remained seated, unlike a gentleman. Well she thought he was seated, but apparently he was standing up to greet her and assist with her seat.

The choice of wine and meal selection was entrusted with Justin, who considered himself an expert in the selection of both.

The evening went well, with some interesting chat, fine wine, excellent cuisine and lots of mutual admiration.

Romance was definitely in the air as they discussed intimate details about their favourite sexual preferences.

Justin intimated he had a real fetish. But, too embarrassed to talk about it, he preferred to fantasise about it instead. However, with the right partner participating, hopefully he could enjoy it during a sexual encounter.

Stella, to her credit, was 'gemme' for anything, so after the third bottle of 1998 Faustino 1 (or should I say, 'El Vino Colapso y Claes Aff') followed by a couple of large brandy chasers, she made it clear in no uncertain terms she was champing at the bit!

They both retired to the hotel suite to finish off their wonderful day, with some romantic, meaningful, old fashioned shagging definitely high on the agenda.

(At this point, it's beginning to sound like a Mills & Boon excerpt, but stay with me here, I'm new to this stuff!)

After doing what you do in the bathroom and before retiring to the alluring super king-size bed, they began with some light petting and kissing, which soon became quite heated as they groped and fondled sensually in the dark for each others private bits!

(Now again at this point, I would warn you if you have a nervous disposition or weak heart. Stop now! . . All those who are sexually aroused and a tad perverted with regards to the outcome, read on!)

The loving foreplay as a starter was wonderful and total eroticism at it's peak. Both participants discovered the finer points of each other's sensual pleasures, while 'sooking' the face off each other.

The bedroom walls were dripping with perspiring, steaming hot passion, as sexual intimacy was on the horizon and careering towards them like a non-stop, out of control, juggernaut with brake failure.

Stella wimpered, moaned and writhed about uncontrollably on the bed with the excitement being whipped up by the occasion!

For old Justin, it was a case of the three 'Gs', groaning, grunting and gagging for it, along with the added sound effects of excessive panting and wheezing, as he groped in the dark exploring every part of her naked body.

Due to the fact that he forgot to pack his asthma inhaler, he stopped every now and again, for a brief moment, while he caught his breath and sprayed some more 'skooshie cream' all over her voluptuous naked breasts to sook.

This was the summit of their sexual encounter. Pleasurable, sexual intercourse personified as they both neared the final target, where they would both experience the ultimate peak in the raw, raucous, off the cuff results, of an enjoyable dirty weekend.

His soft, manly, office worker hands caressing her firm buttocks, began to slowly move their way up her naked, sweaty body and before she knew it, they were cradling her head and face.

She was experiencing pure sexual ecstasy as she neared climax, when Justin suddenly wrapped his hands around her neck and ever so gently (at first) began to squeeze, with his grip firming up and getting tighter and tighter with every passing moment, until it became a fully fledged throttling action.

She called out his name, 'Justin! Justin!' Albeit very muffled and sounding like a grunt, but unfortunately for Stella, it fell on deaf ears as Justin 'the juggernaut' kept plugging away, for want of a better word, and blocking her air supply as he turned into Glesca's equivalent of the 'Boston Strangler' and began to choke the very life out of her.

By now, her eyes were birling around in their sockets, her face was changing colour from an exciteable blushing red, to a desperate bluey, purpley colour, thanks to Justin's improvised tourniquet grip cutting off the oxygen to her lungs.

She struggled uncontrollably to try and talk; every sound she uttered being muffled and sounding like that of the erotic variety to Justin's ears. He responded with rants like, 'Yeah Stella . . . Go for it baby, go for it . . . I knew you would love this!'

Each of his erotic phrases was accompanied by more force being applied to her neck. So much so, that digging her nails fully into his wrists, was equally encouraged with cries of approval, 'Love it Stella! Love it. Now bite my neck at the same time!' It made absolutely no difference to his actions, as he continued in this vein, totally oblivious to her cries of, 'Ye're choking me, ya wee midget bastard!'

Justin was obviously misreading the entire situation, while totally engrossed in his own sexual perversion.

Therefore, the desperate situation called for immediate and drastic action to be taken by Stella, as she went into 'survival police mode'. She released her grip on one of Justin's clamping wrists, slid her hand down rapidly to reach his ready to explode, bulging testicles full of potentially screaming children and ever so gently and promptly, grabbed, stabbed and squeezed them as hard as she could with five beautifully-shaped, long, manicured finger nails. Albeit false, but perfectly made for piercing one's sensitive area of skin.

Surprise! Surprise! That certainly 'nailed' him, as he let out an ear piercing scream that would've shattered a brandy glass. This rush of excruciating pain forced Justin to release his grip on her neck, believing he was having a premature orgasm. However, this false ecstasy was soon rectified when it transpired he now had five, extremely large 'rose' coloured, sharply pointed, false plastic nails decorating his privates. They were left protruding from his rapidly, deflating scrotum or as we say in Glesca, his 'scrawny bawbag', now resembling the latest hedgehog casualty squashed at the side of a busy road.

It was also noticeable that this particular and important piece of his anatomy was also profusely leaking like the rose head on a gardeners watering can, with orphaned 'tadpoles' wriggling about in all directions, after having been so rudely diverted from their original route.

Understandably, Justin's attention was now fully occupied, trying to stem the flow of blood, while delicately pulling the plastic spikes out from his previously bulging scrotum. It now resembled an old fashioned burst football bladder that had just sustained ninety minutes of an Old Firm game.

During this timely distraction, Stella seized the opportunity to grab her clothing and other personal belongings, before 'doing a runner' from the hotel while the going was good. However, this was not before she uttered those infamous words of wisdom, spouted by Ryan O'Neil with great feeling in the film *Love Story*,

'Just remember this Justin, "love means never having to say ye're sorry". Ya wee pervert!'

All this, whilst Justin was still hitting some really high pitched notes that Dame Kiri te Kanawa would have been extremely proud of herself.

Computer dating, who said it was boring?

Finally: what was Paula Yates thinking about when she heard a bang coming from the bedroom next to hers and looked in to see Michael Hutchence hanging from the door with a tie wrapped tightly around his neck and a whole orange stuffed in his mouth.

Translated into 'Gleswegian' for my many readers, it was this:

'Oh come on pizza face! Slacken yer tie aff or ye'll never be able tae swally that orange and ye ken fine well the doacter said fruit wis good for yer acne!'

Flying my Kite

•••

I was in the back garden trying to launch a kite that I'd been given as a Christmas present.

I had followed the instructions to a tee and stuck it all together.

I threw it up in the air and the wind would catch it for a few seconds, then it would come crashing back down to earth.

I persevered with it for a few more times but it would only stay airborne for a few moments.

All the while, my next door neighbour Cathy was watching from her kitchen window, muttering away to herself how all men need to be told how to do everything.

Next thing she opened her window and shouted out to me, 'Ho Harry! I think you need a bit on the side.'

I turned with a confused look on my face and said,

'Not today Cathy, can you not see, I'm trying to fly my kite!'

You're Wanted
• • •

An English force did not have the money to recruit regular police officers, so in order to compensate, the chief constable pushed a recruitment drive through to entice volunteers to enrol.

The special recruitment drive boosted the force numbers.

However, an embarrassing situation arose when a newly recruited Special constable was found to have two outstanding warrants pending for non-payment of fines.

After an interview with a senior officer, it was discovered that when issuing a Fixed Penalty Ticket with the offenders details, he had entered his own name and address by mistake.

Bonk!
• • •

I've just changed the mattress on my marital bed for the new trampoline type.

Mind you . . . I think my wife is going to hit the roof!

Who's Fault!

...

After all the severe heavy snow and frosty weather at the beginning of the year, it's hard to understand what exactly caused it and the damage and mayhem it created for so many people.

During a visit across the city to see my mother, wee Flora, it immediately came up in the conversation, the moment I parked my backside down on her sofa.

'How are you mam?' I asked, and off she went at a tangent.

'How am I? I'll tell ye how I am, I'm bloody fed up and that's jist for starters. Ah mean tae say, whit dae ye make o' this bloody weather, is it no' terrible? We all like tae see a white Christmas but this is over the top,' she said. 'Ah cannae get oot, ah wis meant tae go tae my Arthur-itus club's Christmas dinner last night and big Agnes Broon phoned Isabel next door tae say it wis cancelled . . . Ah've paid my money as well. And Mary Hughes jist phoned me before you came in tae say that the luncheon club's Christmas dinner has been cancelled as well. Some o' the poor auld buggers cannae get oot their hoose . . . Ah'm bloody demented wi' it all (take a breath mam) and yer brother Hughie wis here the other day and cleared my path and look at it noo, it's jist as bad as ever . . .'

'Do you want me to clear the path for you?' I asked.

'Naw! It's jist a disaster, ah feel like a bloody prisoner in my ain hoose. I'm jist demented wi' it Harry . . . Ah cannae even get tae the shops. Isabel next door waited aw day for the Dial-a-Bus, but it never came and she had me doon as her carer, so I was getting on it wi' her.'

'Woah there mam, take a breath.' I said.

'Nae wunner son. Ah feel like an orphan in here masel' and every bloody advert on the telly is aboot sunny beaches, bikinis, warm weather and aw that crap aboot, don't just book it, Peter Cook it.'

'It's Thomas Cook it!' I said.

'Well no' here it's no'. It's icy roads, fur coats, long johns and heavy snow. Ye used tae get the odd wee foxes roaming the streets at night raiding yer bins for a bit o' pizza, or cauld chips. Noo I'm sure I saw a bloody polar bear hunting for stray cats and dugs!'

I tried to explain. 'But the Dial-a-Bus cannae get up the str . . .'

She quickly interrupted me, 'Ah blame aw that lot wi' their arisoles and the damage they dae tae the onion zone.'

I corrected her again, 'It's an aerosol and the Ozone lay . . .'

'Ah know whit it is, ye don't need tae tell me. They've nae respect for any o' us, or the bloody country. Scotland used tae be full of greenery . . . green grass, green trees . . . Crikey, Glesca is known as the Dear Green Place!

Noo, nuthin'. Jist look at the state o' the rainforest for God's sakes, ah've got more trees in my front garden than they have. And where are aw the trees? Fillin' up the bloody shelves in B&Q and Ikea.

Noo look at the place, the jungle looks like a desert and all the people that lived there have moved intae a Glesca homeless unit . . . Everywhere ye look, it's one disaster efter another, the telly is full of it.

'Mam! You've lost the plot.' I said. 'One minute you're

talking about the snow and ice and how you can't get out to your clubs and next minute, you're the female version of Al Gore and sounding off like an Eco-warrior . . .'

'Don't dare make excuses for this government and as for that Alex Salmon! He isnae much better. Ah bet ye the streets and roads through in Edinburgh are all clear.

'You're right there mam, there's definitely something fishy about Alex Salmond.' I responded.

'It's nothing but repeats on that telly as well. *The Towering Inferno*, *Earthquake* and *Armageddon*, every one a disaster movie, and at Christmas tae. Thank goodness for *Corrie* and *Emmerdale* to bring a bit of normality intae yer life or the telly would be full o' they bloody disaster movies.'

At that, the door bell wrang.

'That'll be my wee paperboy for his money . . . Here,' she said, handing me some money. 'Gie him an extra fiver tip, he never lets me down. Rain, hail or snaw. That wean paps a paper through my door.'

With that description of loyalty wringing in my ears, I went to the front door and paid the paperboy. On my return, she was totally engrossed, watching, *War of the Worlds* on television.

'Here's your paper mam. Do you want a cuppa tea? Do ye want anything from the shops? Machine gun, army tank . . . Anything?' I asked.

'Aye! You tae shut up and let me watch this in peace. Ye've no' stopped talking since ye came in! . . . Nae offence son, but I like that wee Tom Cruise . . . might be a wee midget, but a definite looker!'

'Well I'll leave you to watch it then, mam. I'll phone you later to see who won the war.'

As I was leaving, she shouted out after me, 'Remember and don't phone me when *Corrie*'s on son, there's a big train crash tonight and I don't want tae miss it! Promises tae be good .. there's a lot o' the auld yins getting killed off! They could dae wi' a good clear out.'

Double Take
...

In some of my earlier books, I've often mentioned my good friend and former colleague Stevie Mack. Instantly recogniseable because he was a big, good looking black police officer.

We would regularly, jokingly, inform people that we were twins.

The difficulty convincing people, was with me being as white as a ghost and him as black as two in the morning, but it was just a laugh.

However, at a police night out a certain force station assistant, slightly the worse off for drink, said in all seriousness, 'How can you possibly be twins?'

I looked at him with a puzzled expression on my face, trying to think up a funny reply, when he then blurted out, to everyone's amusement.

'For a start. You've got different surnames!'

Not exactly the most obvious difference you'd notice first, surely!

Anything You Say

· · ·

If you've ever worked with a boss who reacts before getting all the facts and thinking things through, you will love this!

Morris & Morrison Carpets, decided it was time for a shake up within the company and, as a result, they hired ex-police chief superintendent Henderson as their new chief executive officer.

The new chief was determined to impose his authority and rid the company of all slackers. Therefore, while on a tour of the factory, he noticed a young guy leaning against a stack of carpets. With the room full of workers, he wanted to make them all aware that he meant business. He started by asking the young guy, 'How much money do you earn in a week son?'

Slightly surprised by the question, the young guy looked at him and replied, 'It depends, but usually between £140 and £160 a week. Why do you ask sir?'

The chief said, 'For a reason. Now just wait right here and don't move.' He walked back to his office, returned within a few minutes, and handed the young guy £640 in cash and said, 'Here's four weeks wages for you. Now leave the factory and don't come back.'

The young guy gratefully accepted the money and left without a word.

Feeling pretty good about himself the chief looked around the room and asked, 'Does anyone wish to enlighten me as to what that young layabout did here?'

To which a worker called out from across the room, 'Nuthin! He was the pizza delivery guy from Domino's.'

Drink up!

• • •

There was this wee Glesca punter, sitting on a stool at the bar, staring at the drink in front of him, when a big, trouble-making bully walked up to him. He grabbed the whisky glass sitting in front of him and gulped it down in one swig.

'Well mister dipstick, what ye gonnae dae about that then?' He said menacingly, as the wee Glesca punter promptly burst into tears.

'Come on, greetin' face.' The bully said, 'I didnae take you for a cry baby. I cannae stand tae see a grown man crying, noo chuck it ya wee wimp.'

'Well you'd cry too, if you were me. This has been the worst day of my life.' He said. 'I'm a complete and utter failure . . .

'I arrived late for a company meeting and my boss fired me.

'Then when I went to the car park, I discovered my car had been stolen and I don't have any insurance for it . . .

'Then I lost my wallet and had to get a bus home.

'I arrived home and found my wife in bed with the next door neighbour . . .

'As I went to leave the house, my dog attacked me and bit my arm.

'I was so totally fed up with life, that I came to this bar to work up enough courage to put an end to it all . . .

'I bought myself a strong drink and I dropped a cyanide capsule into it and was sitting, patiently waiting for the poison to dissolve. When you, ya big arsehole, had to butt in and drink the whole lot down for me!'

(He paused for a moment, before continuing)

'However, enough about me. How is your day going big man?'

Don't Ask

. . .

A policewoman called her shift inspector one morning and told him that she was staying at home because she was not feeling very well.

'What's the matter with you?' He asked her.

'I have a serious case of anal glaucoma!' She said in a weak voice.

'What the hell is anal glaucoma?' He asked.

To which she replied, 'It's when you can't see yourself being arsed about going into work today. That's what!'

Organic White Tea

...

A woman went to seek advice from her local community police constable, about getting physically abused on a weekly basis by her drunken husband.

'How did you get the bruises on your face?' He asked her.

'It was my husband. He does it every time he comes home drunk, he beats me to a pulp. I just don't know what to do about it.'

'Well I have a really good remedy for that. Next time your husband comes home drunk, just make a cup of organic white tea and start swishing it about your mouth. Swish and swish but whatever you do, don't swallow it, until he goes to bed and falls asleep.'

Two weeks later the woman returned to see the community cop, looking fresh, reborn with not a blemish on her face.

'I just wanted to say officer, that was a brilliant idea of yours, that every time my husband came home with a drink in him, to swish with organic white tea. I swished and swished and he never touched me once!'

To which the Community cop replied, 'See how much of a difference it makes keeping your mouth shut?'

Glesca Polis at their Best

• • •

I was saddened to learn recently about the sudden death of my former police colleague Alex Craig.

Alex was what we would describe as a real character and I know that personally because he sent me several funny anecdotes over the years. I was delighted to include a few of those involving him in my 'Harry the Polis' series of books and he would always finish off his wee story with, 'Glesca polis at their best'.

Another colleague of mine and Alex, Maggie Mulligan, sent me this anecdote of an incident that involved both of them.

They received a call that there was a housebreaker in a partially derelict building in Trongate.

Along with Alex and Willie Robertson, they attended and on their arrival outside, Maggie, being the youngest and fittest, entered the building first and climbed up the dodgy stairway. Once inside she saw the ned – a young guy, roughly her age – standing at the other end of a big, empty, rundown warehouse, with holes all over the loose floorboards.

Maggie started to lightly prance across the loose floorboards like a Bolshoi ballerina towards him, when halfway across, the young ned turned and shouted out, 'Oh hen! Be careful there, or ye'll go right through the floor, it's just gyp rock! Real cheap shite.'

After passing on this information, he then turned around and ran off down the opposite staircase at his side of the building.

As she stood there deciding her next move, she heard Alex voice behind her shouting, 'Well whit are ye waiting for Maggie? An invitation! Get after the bastard or he'll get away!'

With these 'words of wisdom', ringing out in her ears, she cautiously but nimbly, pursued him across the gyp rock flooring, not caring a jot about his warning, or the consequences.

After successfully negotiating the loose flooring, Maggie continued to give chase after him along the Trongate, when suddenly the young ned stopped and turned around to face her with his hands up.

'Och for fuxsakes hen, ah gie up. I'll jist come wae ye,' he said, offering up his wrists to be handcuffed.

Up until this point, Maggie had never properly handcuffed anyone so she reached out and took his hand and nice as you like, she walked him back to the derelict building like a young courting couple, much to the guffaws of her mature, male colleagues, Alex and Willie.

The thing was, when they got to the charge bar and of course the whole squad wanted a 'speakie part in the case', Maggie was politely told to 'go and put the kettle on hen and make a cup o' tea'.

During her absence, when the officer on duty asked who were the arresting officers, Alex spoke up and graciously responded, 'Well, to be perfectly honest Inspector, it was Maggie the young lassie who caught him on her own.' Much to the horror and disdain of the older cops in the squad, who regarded Maggie as a 'wee decorative polis wummin', just out the new wrapper and as a result, not ready to be trusted as a serious witness for court.

Maggie let it pass, after all, it was hardly the crime of the century at that stage of her career.

However, she never forgot that Alex did speak up for her and she always gave him a knowing smile from that day, until he retired.

Finally, a wee quickie . . . the last time I spoke with Alex over the phone about the old times, he was telling me a story from the job and finished off with, 'Ye know me Harry! When duty called, I was always at the front of the queue.'

To which I couldn't resist adding, 'Aye! In the front of the queue in the chip shop Alex!'

'Glesca polis at their best!'

Gone, but certainly not forgotten.

Lucky White Heather

...

A young man was sitting on a blanket at Helensburgh beach. He had no arms and no legs.

Three women out for a day at the beach, from England, Wales and Scotland, were walking past and felt sorry for him lying there.

The English woman said, 'Have you ever had a hug?'

The young man replied, 'No missus!'

So the English woman went over and gave him a hug before walking on.

The Welsh woman stepped forward and said, 'Have you ever had a kiss?'

The young man said, 'Never!'

At that, the Welsh woman stepped forward and she gave him a long passionate kiss. After which, she walked off.

The wee Scottish woman came up to him and said, 'Here son, huv ye ever been screwed?'

The young man's expression broke into a big smile and he replied, 'No missus, ah huvnae!'

To which she replied, 'Well, ye will be very shortly when that tide comes in!'

The Lingo

• • •

Five Germans in an Audi Quattro are driving around Spain when they are stopped by the Guardia Civil.

The Guardia Civil Officer tells them, 'It'sa illegala to putta cinco personas in a Quattro, si?'

'Vot dos you mean eet's illegal?' Asked the German driver.

'Well Quattro meansa four.' Replied the Guardia official.

'Quattro is just ze name of zeblutten automobile'. The German driver replied. 'Vill you look at ze dam registration papers, ze car is designed to carry five persons.'

'You canta pulla thata uno on me por favor!' Replied the Guardia police officer. 'Quattro meansa four, si? You have cinco, five personas ina your car and you are thereforea breaking the Spanish law.'

The German driver replied angrily, 'You idiot! Call your zupervisor over. I vant to speak to someone viz more intelligence than you!'

'Sorry signor!' Responded the Guardia Civil officer, 'He can'ta come over. He'sa busy witha dos, two signors in a Fiat Uno.'

Groggery Speck!

. . .

My wee mother Flo was an amazing wee wummin, who had a great cure for everything. Call it an old wife's tale or what, she had her own special remedy for every situation. The following are some examples:

'Aw mammy, I've had a nose bleed and it's all over my school shirt. How will I get the red stain out of it?'

My mother quickly pulled me over to her, 'grogged' into her hand and rubbed it all over the blood stain. Blood stain gone . . .

My brother Allan was leaving for the school one morning and his hair was sticking straight up in the air like a 'cow's lick'. My mother quickly pulled him over to her, 'grogged' into her hand and patted his hair down. Cow's lick gone . . .

My brother Hugh came in one day shouting and screaming, 'Ah mammy, I've broken my ankle.' The bone was literally sticking out from his foot at right angles.

'Let me see it, son'. Said my mam, as she pulled him over to her, 'grogged' into her hand and rubbed his ankle. 'There ye go son, ye're awright!' Broken ankle gone . . .

My brother Freddie awoke one morning for school with the start of a stye. 'Mammy, I've got a right sore eye.'

'Let me see it, son'. Said my mam, as she pulled him over to her, 'grogged' into her hand and rubbed his eye. 'There ye go son, ye're awright!' Sore eye . . . worse!

My poor brother had to wear a pair of brown John Lennon glasses, before they were fashionable all through his school years, with a pink elastoplast plaster strip over the lens of his right eye.

To this day, even the magical wonders of computer technology and that of Photoshop can't alter the picture. Totally ruined his wedding photos!

Who said that the auld wifey remedy cures were the best, Persil, Brylcreem, Florence Nightingale or Specsavers? . . . I don't think so!

The Cubicle
• • •

It's funny how something as sacred as a church can trigger off a wee funny story that you heard years ago. This one is about an old drunken man who wandered into a church and entered a confessional box. He sat there for a few moments in silence, so the priest coughed to get his attention but the old drunken man ignored him and continued to sit there in silence. A few moments later, the priest coughed again, only this time it was a bit louder. However, the old drunk continued to ignore him. Running out of patience, the priest knocked on the partition of the confessional box, in an attempt to get the drunken man's attention. At this annoyance, the drunken man blurted out, 'Ho! It's no use knocking on my door mate, there's nae toilet paper in here either!'

Doctor! Doctor!

· · ·

An elderly woman went to the doctor's office where she was seen by one of the younger doctors.

After about four minutes into the examination, the door was thrown open and she burst out of the room screaming, as she ran down the hall.

A senior doctor stopped her and asked what the problem was and she told him her story.

After listening to what she had to say, he had her sit down and relax in another room.

The senior doctor marched down the hallway back to the examination room, where the young doctor was writing away on his clipboard.

'What's the matter with you?' The senior doctor demanded to know, 'Missus Smith is sixty-two years old, she has five grown up children and six grandchildren, and you've just told her that she's pregnant?'

The younger doctor continued writing on his clipboard and without looking up said, 'Does she still have the hiccups?'

PC Illiterate

• • •

This is a true story sent to me by a friend who works with a Computer Support System Company

'Hello, Computer Support Systems, can I help you?'

'Aye hello there mate, ah'll tell ye whit it is, right! Um having trouble wi' my computer. It's a brand new shot! Know whit a mean?'

'What kind of trouble are you experiencing?'

'Well, I was dayin' the auld wan finger typing thing, right, and all of a sudden the words ah wis writing jist disappeared aff the screen.'

'The letters you were typing went away?'

'Correcto! But it wisnae really letters mate, it wis jist a wee story for the weans but, as God is my judge mate, they jist disappeared.'

'So what have you got up on your screen at the moment?'

'Nothing mate. No' even the weans screensaver picture o' Shrek . . . Zilch!'

'There's nothing at all?'

'That's whit am tellin' ye mate. It's totally "blankety blank", as auld Terry Wogan would say. It'll no' dae a thing when I type. I've even tried typing my name hunners o' times.'

'Are you still in Word or did you get out of it?'

'How would I know that mate? . . . Whit word ur ye talking aboot?'

'Well can you see a 'C' prompt on your screen?'

'Whit's a sea-prompt mate?'

'Never mind, can you move your cursor around the screen?'

'There isnae any cursor here I telt ye, it wullnae dae anything.'

'Does your monitor have a power indicator on it?'

'Ye're asking me aw these hi-tech questions mate, but whit is the monitor?'

'The monitor's the screen you're looking at that looks like a TV. Does it have a light that tells you when it's switched on?'

'Ah don't know. Dae you no' know yersel'.

'No sir, I don't. I can't see it.'

'That's two o' us mate. Ah cannae see it either'.

'Well, take a look at the back of the monitor, that's the TV screen, and see where the power cable goes into it. Can you see that?'

'Aye mate, I think so. It's grey in't it?'

'Probably. Now follow the cable to the plug and tell me if it's plugged into the wall.'

'Aye, it's plugged in, mate. Ah can feel it.'

'Now, see when you were behind the monitor, did you notice if there were maybe two cables plugged into the back of it?'

'Naw mate. I didnae notice that.'

'Well, there usually are. So I need you to look behind it again and find the other cable for me.'

'Okay mate. Here it is. I've found it'

'Right! Now I want you to follow it for me, and tell me if it's plugged into the back of your computer.'

'Ah cannae reach it.'

'Well, can you just look and see if it is plugged in?'

'Naw mate, ah cannae. I'm stretching as it is.'

'Can you maybe put your knee on something and lean over and check it?'

'Haud oan. I'll need tae move the weans bike oot the road.'

(There's a moment's pause)

'Have you done that yet?'

'Right, I've done it.'

'Now can you see if it's plugged in?'

'Naw mate. Ah still cannae see it right, because it's dark in here.'

'Did you say it was dark?'

'Dark! It's as black as two in the morning mate, I'm groping aboot in the dark. Wait and I'll see if I can find the weans torch. There's nae lights on in the hoose anywhere.

'Well, why don't you just turn on the house lights then.'

'Ah cannae mate!'

'And why not?'

'Cause the 'lecky's been cut aff.'

'So you have no electricity in the house?'

'That's whit I'm trying tae tell ye mate, Scottish Power cut it aff yesterday!'

'Okay, I think I know what your problem is. Do you still have the computer boxes, manuals and packaging stuff your computer came in?'

'Aye mate. It's pure brand new.'

'Good. Well go and look them out, unplug your computer system and pack it back into the boxes just like it was when you got it. Then take it right back to the store where you bought it from and ask for your money back!'

'Really? Is the problem that bad mate?'

'Yes, I'm afraid it is that bad, mate.'

'So whit dae ah tell them is wrang wi' it then?'

'Simple! You tell them that you're too fucken stupid to own a computer and could they please take it back!'

At that, the Help Desk advisor slammed the phone down!

(There was a short pause, before the wee Glesca ned said)

'Will they know whit a mean, mate?

'Helloooooo . . .

'Ur ye still there mate?'

Holy Whit!

· · ·

Father Gilhooley awoke from his bed one morning and looked out the parochial house window at a beautiful spring morning in his new Cumbernauld parish in Scotland.

He walked to the front door to get a deep breath of the beautiful day outside, when he noticed there was a dead donkey lying in the middle of his front lawn.

This was an unusual sight to behold and not knowing who else to inform about it, he promptly contacted the local police station.

The conversation went like this:

'Good morning, Strathclyde police, Cumbernauld, Sergeant Jones speaking. How might I help you?'

'And the best of the day ter yer good self, sergeant. This is Father Gilhooley at St Francis Catholic Church. There's a dead donkey lying right in der middle of me front lawn at the house.'

Sergeant Jones, who considered himself to be quite a witty character, replied with a smirk, 'Well now Father, it was always my impression that you Catholic priests were the right people for taking care of the last rites!'

There was dead silence on the line for a long moment and then Father Gilhooley replied,

'Ah, to be sure Sergeant Jones, that would be correct, but we are also obliged to notify the next of kin first!'

Porky & Best

...

One of the biggest advantages for the county forces being part of Strathclyde Police was the bulk buying of police vehicles.

However this centralised system gave absolutely no thought to geography and so it came to pass on the 14 February at Kames, in Tighnabruaich, the old faithful and trusted Ford Escort 'panda' was replaced by a small Mini Metro 'panda'.

Now big Davy Best, the local polis driver was over six feet in height, but in fairness to the car it took him to places that the old faithful Escort couldn't.

On one occasion, Davy was heading towards Dunoon and was about twenty-five miles away on a mainly single track road, when he drove round a bend to discover the road blocked by a huge pig standing there.

Despite it being bigger than the police mini Metro, Davy got out and tried the friendly approach to shoo it away. However, this failed miserably, due to the pig being overly friendly and a tad amorous.

So Davy jumped back into the Metro and attempted to drive off but the lovesick pig was having none of it and became quite excited. It began rubbing itself along the front of the car and trying to mount it.

Eventually, as it moved around to one side of the car to try for a better position, Davy seized the opportunity to drive off as fast as the Metro could go.

Unfazed by this manoeuvre, the pig was not too enamoured about losing its new friend and decided to give chase after the Metro for about quarter of a mile before giving in to the Metro's superior 'horse power'.

If only we had the police helicopter with its TV cameras then, I'm sure Harry Hill viewers would have loved the footage of the 'Valentine's Day Love Sick Pig'.

Davy never did mention if the pig found his own Miss Piggy or was waiting for him on his return journey.

Then again, maybe he just chickened out and left his pig sick admirer to stop acting the goat and get over it!

Second Wife Syndrome
. . .

I was in Marks & Spencers one day, when I bumped into an ex-inspector whom I had worked with but didn't particularly get on with during our time together.

'Oh hi Harry. Still writing those silly wee books of yours or have you got a proper job at last?' He said.

'I'm still writing my wee books, Jim. Much better than working for a living!' I replied.

Just at that, a woman sitting at a table nearby waved over to him prompting him to respond and wave back.

'That's Debbie.' He announced, 'She's my second wife.'

At this point, I couldn't resist saying it, 'Your second wife!' I said, pausing for a moment . . .

'I've got to agree with you Jim . . . She wouldn't have been my first choice either!'

At that, I walked off leaving him to contemplate what I had just said.

Teleprinters

...

In the early days of the '70s before computers, all messages would arrive at the police stations by telex, like a ticker-tape teleprinter.

Up in Oban, the Sub-Divisional Officer (SDO) would indicate that he had read a telex message by ticking the corner with a pen.

Every morning about 6am the Glasgow Weather Centre would send out the forecast for the day.

Being bored on the nightshift and with plenty of time on his hands, the office man switched the telex machine on to a local setting and typed out a spoof weather report.

This message read, 'Due to unforseen industrial action being implemented by the staff at the Meteorological Office in Glasgow, there will be a repeat of yesterday's weather.'

The following night, on checking his spoof telex report, he saw that the SDO had ticked it, thereby confirming he had read it.

So the office man decided to take it a step further and made up another spoof weather report to submit.

This one read, 'There will be weather all over the country today. Following a return to work after their twenty-four hour dispute, the Meteorological Office staff in Glasgow have decided to have a good weather day, everywhere. Enjoy!'

Yes, you've guessed it. The SDO ticked it off.

Makes you wonder what other reports he didn't bother to read!

Wear O' Ware

· · ·

One evening, a close friend of the Divisional Commander of Dumbarton police headquarters had his car broken into and contacted the boss personally about it.

The boss immediately passed it on to the shift inspector to inform the shift going on duty to keep a look out for the easily identifiable items stolen.

In particular, a pair of white training shoes and a blue and white coloured jumper.

Now the training shoes were a new thing back in the early '70s, so when two beat cops noticed a well known local ned wearing a shiny new pair of white trainers, it didn't need the divisional CID to solve the case.

The ned was placed in the detention room waiting to be charged, when the boss, on hearing about the arrest of the accused, decided to poke his nose into the enquiry.

He entered the CID room just as the production labels were being tied to the white training shoes.

'So these are the training shoes he stole?' He asked.

'Yes boss, he had them on.' Replied one of the cops.

'And what about the jumper?' Said the boss.

'I put it to him boss, but he wisnae wearing it!' Replied the cop.

'To which the boss blew a fuse and ranted, 'It's bloody obvious that he wasn't wearing it or he'd still have it on!' Sometimes bosses are better staying in their wee offices and leave the cops to deal with the crimes . . .

Cause we know what we're talking about!

Workmate

· · ·

It was with great sadness that I recently learned of the death of Ron Hickman, the genius who gave the world the amazing DIY phenomenon, the Workmate.

This could be bought in every B&Q store and came in a very small flat pack box, approximately 18" x 18" and opened up into a joiners work-bench fitted with metal legs, vices for holding items, measuring equipment and mitre saw frame.

It was a complete revelation for all DIY enthusiasts and professionals.

However, I was surprised to hear that he was buried in a standard size coffin and not folded up and put away in one of his Workmate boxes . . .

Well let's be honest, it would have made more sense to me!

Trapped by the Goolies!

• • •

Whilst in Spain recently, I was sitting at the beach bar when a man seated next to me told me the following story.

He told me about a private nudist beach area, not far away, where one of the young male nudists got an unexpected, nasty surprise. When he tried to get up from his sun lounger, he discovered he was trapped by the balls.

Apparently, he was a member of this private nudist colony. He had been in the sea swimming about naked for some time, then, when he came out of the water and sat down on his sun lounger, his testicles slipped through the slats.

As he lay there sunbathing, unaware that his testicles were now dangling, they expanded back to normal size with the heat of the sun and became stuck in between the slats of his sun lounger.

It wasn't until some friends asked him if he was going for a beer, that he discovered his plight!

(My eyes are watering at this bit guys!)

Fortunately for him, he was freed a short time later by a maintenance service man, who just happened to be passing (Aye right!) and saw what had happened.

The passing joiner managed to saw a few slats of the sun lounger and free its very embarrassed victim . . . To go for a beer!

And no doubt, to have his embarrassing incident broadcast and viewed 2,894,762 times on YouTube!

Pure quality filming! I heard.

I See Nuthin'!

...

Old Des Smith (nicknamed Granny) was a really decent cop who was promoted late in his service and got posted to Lochgilphead in the Argyll area of Strathclyde.

Unfortunately, for someone who was on the down slope of his service and looking for an easy, trouble free, last few years, it changed him completely. Suddenly he had inherited a shift of younger men, unlike himself and was determined that he was going to sort them out.

During one particular backshift Les Fraser, one of the shift cops, was rallying the police 'panda' along a forest road above Ardrishaig. As he came around the bend, he found the road blocked by forestry works and tree felling.

He immediately took evasive action and braked, whereby the 'panda' skidded, spun around and slid sideways along the road, eventually coming to rest in a deep ditch.

Fortunately, he was not injured and no visible damage was done to the panda but it was well and truly stuck in the muddy ditch.

Being a wise and resourceful officer, Les looked around for a solution to his problem and located a mobile crane nearby, which was being used by the Forestry Commission.

As luck would have it, the ignition keys for the crane were hidden under the operator's seat.

Les jumped into the cab, started the engine and proceded to operate the crane, hitching the long leather straps attached to it under the police 'panda'.

Meanwhile, Granny Smith, the sergeant, was out driving about the area on his own and getting acquainted with his new surroundings, when he saw a car's headlights in the forest and decided to investigate.

Suffice to say he got the biggest shock of his short police career as a sergeant, when he drove around the bend and saw the mobile crane, being operated by the polis, with a police 'panda' car dangling in the air from the end of it!

On seeing the sergeant looking on disbelievingly, Les nonchalantly gave him the thumbs up, as if this was normal practice.

Whereby Granny casually waved back at him, before promptly reversing out of the forest and driving off in the opposite direction!

Terrorist Attack

• • •

One evening, Ricky Gault received an urgent call instructing him to attend at Graham's Point on the Holy Loch, regarding a report of a suspected Al-Qaeda terrorist attack being launched against the US naval base!

Apparently the on duty watch commander of the USS Simon Lake had observed two suspects nearby, setting fire to an object and sending it off in the direction of the ship.

Ricky arrived at the location within minutes to discover an elderly local man and his grandson holding a mock Viking funeral for his recently deceased pet guinea pig.

Ricky subsequently cancelled all other police stations attending the incident, referring to the suspected terrorist attack in his report as being 'Friendly fire observed at the scene. No police action!'

Parrot Patter

. . .

An elderly woman goes to see her parish priest one day and says, 'Excuse me Father, but I'm looking for some advice on a problem.

'You see, I have two female pet parrots that talk but they only ever say one thing and it's very embarrassing.'

'And what would that be, missus Brown?' Asked the parish priest.

'Well they both say, "Hi there, we're a couple of hookers! Do you want to have some fun?"'

'That's totally obscene!' The priest exclaimed. Then he paused for a brief moment . . .

'You know, missus Brown.' He said, 'I just might have an answer to your problem. You see, I have two male talking parrots, which I have taught to pray and read the Bible ever since they were hatched . . .

'Why don't you bring your two parrots over to the chapel house and we'll put them into the same cage with my Francis and Peter. Maybe my parrots can convert your parrots and teach them to pray and worship, so they stop saying that totally obscene and embarrassing phrase.'

'Oh thank you Father,' the elderly woman replied, 'this just might be the ideal solution for them.'

The following day, the elderly woman brought her two female parrots to the priest's house. As he invited her in, she immediately saw his two male parrots inside their cage holding rosary beads in one foot and praying.

Impressed with what she was seeing, she walked over and put her parrots in the cage with them.

After a few minutes, the female parrots cried out in unison,

'Hi, we're hookers! Do you want to have some fun?'

There was stunned silence . . .

Shocked by their introduction, one male parrot looked over at the other male parrot and said, 'Put the beads away Frankie boy, I think our prayers have finally been answered!'

I Know You!

. . .

A policeman notices an attractive young woman staring at him and smiling in the supermarket and can't resist talking to her, 'Sorry, but do I know you?'

She replied, 'I think so, aren't you the father of one of my children?' He quickly thinks back to the only time he was ever unfaithful and the penny dropped, 'Were you the nurse that I had mad passionate sex with on the snooker table at my stag do?'

'No!' she replied, shaking her head in embarrassment. 'I certainly am not . . . I'm your daughter's primary school teacher!'

Be a Sport

. . .

Which reminds me of the young policeman who was out one night at a retiral do in the police social club when he pulled an older woman.

She was a fifty-eight year old female turnkey and single parent but looked pretty good for her age.

On the way back to her house, the young cop started fantasising, thinking, mmmm! If her daughter looks anything like her, I bet she is really hot! When suddenly, out of the blue, the woman asked him if he would like a Sportsman's Double?

'What's that?' He asked.

'It's a mother and daughter threesome!' She replied.

'Wow!! Yes please!' He answered excitedly.

So as they entered her front door, she switched on the hall light and shouted, 'Mum! Are you still awake?!'

Come Quick

· · ·

My sister Linda works as a controller for the emergency services and received a call from an irate woman, it went like this:

'Emergency services, which service do you require?'

'Send the fire brigade quickly! My hoose is oan fire, the flames are everywhere!'

Linda replied, 'Okay madam, so how do we get there?' She asked.

There was a moments silence, before the woman caller replied sarcastically . . . 'Daw! Ye come in yer big friggin' red fire truck!!'

Pastoral News

· · ·

A wee Glesca boy was sitting, waiting for his mammy to come out of a grocery store. While sitting there, he was approached by a man who asked, 'Excuse me son, can you tell me where the Post Office is?'

The wee boy replied, 'Aye nae bother! Just go straight down this road and turn tae yer right.'

The man thanked the wee boy kindly and said, 'I'm the new minister in Castlemilk. I'd love you to come to church on Sunday and if you do, I'll show you how to get to Heaven.'

The wee boy laughed and said. 'Awe gie's a break big man! You don't even know how tae get tae the Post Office . . . Never mind heaven!'

Computers R Us

· · ·

Mister Armstrong was a store manager for Computers R Us in Little Rock, St Louis, USA, who contacted the police informing them that he was detaining a thief within his store.

On their arrival, he informed the police officers he'd observed the male customer, later identified as Tyrone Jackson of Arkansas, on his surveillance camera, concealing a silver coloured laptop computer under his hoodie jacket.

When confronted, the accused Jackson became very abusive, pushed an employee of the store, pulled out a knife and threatened him with it, before making a run for the door.

Unfortunately for Jackson, outside on the street were four US marines collecting toys for the 'Toys for Tots' charity. Mister Armstrong said, on hearing his shout for help, the four marines stopped Jackson as he tried to leave the store.

A struggle took place, whereby Jackson stabbed one of the marines, Cpl Aaron Hodge, in the back. Fortunately, the injury sustained was not life threatening.

After the police and an ambulance arrived at the scene of the incident, Cpl Hodge was conveyed to the hospital for treatment. Along with the accused Jackson, who sustained two broken arms, a broken ankle, a broken leg, several missing teeth, possible broken ribs, multiple contusions, assorted lacerations, a broken nose and a broken jaw.

All injuries he sustained when he slipped and fell backwards off of the kerb, after stabbing Cpl Hodge of the US Marine Corp.

Having been to America, all I would say is, I'm not surprised. They do have some very nasty high kerbs there!

Now that was what you call a well-written police report.

PC Tips

• • •

Wouldn't it be nice if every time we mucked up our life, we could simply press 'Ctrl-Alt-Delete' and just start all over again?

Too easy!

Norah Batty

...

A wee Glesca punter was washed up on a beach after being shipwrecked.

The only other survivors were a ewe and a sheepdog.

After looking around, he realised that they were stranded on a deserted island.

After being there for a while, he got into the habit of taking his two animal companions to the beach every evening to watch the sunset.

One particular evening, the sky was a fiery red with beautiful cirrus clouds, the breeze was warm and gentle; the perfect night for romance . . .

As they sat there looking out to sea, the ewe started looking better and better to the lonely man.

Soon, he leaned over to it and put his arm around its neck.

The sheepdog, ever protective of the ewe, growled fiercely until the man took his arm away.

After that the three of them continued to enjoy the sunsets together but there was no more cuddling.

Several weeks later, lo and behold, there was another shipwreck.

The only survivor was Norah Batty. That evening, the man invited Norah along to the evening beach ritual.

It was another beautiful evening, with a red sky, cirrus clouds, a warm gentle breeze and perfect conditions for a night of romance.

Pretty soon, the man started to get those feelings again.

He fought the urges as long as he could but he finally gave in and leaned over to Norah and told her he hadn't had sex for months.

Norah batted her eyelashes and asked if there was anything she could do for him.

'Aye!' he replied, 'Ye could take that bloody dog for a walk.'

Whit?
· · ·

I loved this play on accents when I first heard it.

A Yorkshire man takes his cat to a vet surgery and says in his broad accent,

'Ay up lad, I need to talk with thee about me cat.'

'Is it a tom?' Enquired the vet.

To which he responded, 'Nay lad, it's in thee car outside.'

Four Worms!

· · ·

A young community policeman decided that a visual demonstration of his 'lesson to be learned', would add emphasis to his talk to the kids at a local primary school.

He placed four worms into four separate jars.

The first worm was put into a container filled with alcohol.

The second worm was put into a container filled with cigarette smoke.

The third worm was put into a container filled with chocolate syrup.

And the fourth worm was put into a container filled with good clean soil.

At the conclusion of his talk, the young policeman informed the school children of the following results; holding the worms up, one at a time for them all to see.

The first worm soaked in the alcohol jar was Dead!

The second worm in the cigarette smoke filled jar was Dead!

The third worm, smothered in the chocolate syrup was Dead!

Finally, the fourth worm in the good clean soil was still Alive!

The young officer asked the children in the classroom, 'So, who can tell me, what lesson did you learn from the demonstration this morning?'

Wee Madonna McGinn, who was sitting at the back of the class, quickly raised her hand.

'The girl at the back with the red striped skirt.' He said. 'Tell us all the lesson we should learn from this demonstration.'

To which she replied, 'As long as you continue tae drink, smoke and eat chocolate, ye wullnae get worms!'

Gone Fishing
. . .

Strathclyde police fishing section were holding a fishing competition near a bridge in Paisley, when suddenly a funeral cortege of cars drove over the bridge.

On seeing this, one of the older police officers jumped to his feet, removed his bunnet and bowed his head as a mark of respect.

When the cars had passed he put his bunnet back on, sat back down and carried on with his fishing.

His partner, fishing next to him turned and said, 'Here Davie, that's one of the nicest, most respectful things I've ever seen you do.'

Davie replied, 'Well after all, we were married for nearly twenty years!'

Choking!

. . .

A woman sitting in the police social club suddenly began to cough.

After a few seconds it became apparent that she was in real distress.

Fortunately, big Donnie Henderson, sitting at the next table turned to look at her.

'Whit's up wi' ye hen? Can ye no' swally?'

The distressed woman signalled, 'No!' by desperately shaking her head from side to side.

'Can ye no' breathe either?' Asked Donnie. The woman shook her head more vigorously. 'No!'

Her face was turning from red to blue.

That said, Donnie casually walked up behind her, lifted up the back of her dress, pulled down her pants and licked her bare bum.

This action totally shocked the woman into such a violent spasm that the obstruction choking her, flew out of her mouth and she began to breathe normally again.

At that, Donnie nonchalantly swaggered back to his table, downed a glass of whisky straight down then loudly announced to an astonished police social club crowd looking on.

And that, my friends, is known as the 'hind-lick manoeuvre!'

Hulk Hogan Calling

• • •

There was I, along with my wife Marion, enjoying our first trip to the home of country music, Nashville Tenessee.

Johnny Cash, Willie Nelson, Garth Brooks, Loretta Lynn, Patsy Cline, you name the country legend and they'll have graced the Grand Ole Opry in Nashville at one time or another.

With this in mind, we both looked forward to seeing, hearing and if we were very lucky, maybe meeting some of the old and new generation of country music stars established or coming through. Such as Travis Mann, Jimmy Buffet, Dusty Hundley, Charlie Daniels, Jimmy Ruiz, to name but a few.

We were excited about our trip and the possible prospect. So you can imagine my surprise when one evening, upon walking into my hotel, I literally bumped into the WWF wrestler and reality TV star, big Hulk Hogan!

Decked out in a bright red bandana, dark sunglasses, bright red t-shirt, denim jeans and black Nike boot trainers with a flip-top mobile phone stuck to his right ear, talking away. Oh, and a very noticeable limp.

Yes, Hulk Hogan, not exactly the first celebrity name I expected to meet in Nashville but like all celebrities you see regularly on the big screen or TV, you immediately believe that you know them personally. Being totally surprised by my unexpected 'meeting', I instinctively greeted him with, 'Hiya Hulk, any chance of a wee photo together?'

At which point he allowed himself a fleeting glance in my direction, as he tried to decipher what language I was talking and which planet had I just been to, before arriving on earth.

Realising I had blurted this request out, while he appeared to be engaged in conversation with someone on the phone, I politely backed off.

That said, he continued talking and walking outside and got into a big four-by-four and quickly drove off.

However, during this brief spell in his presence, I did manage to reel off a few photos of him to prove to Marion that I hadn't overstayed my allocated Happy Hour period in the bar.

Marion immediately responded with, 'That's an old trick. Sticking a phone to your ear and pretending to be engaged in conversation so you can ignore people! I'm surprised you fell for that one.'

Later that evening, on our way out for dinner, lo and behold, here he was again, walking through the hotel lobby. He was dressed in the same attire, with the flip-top mobile phone stuck to his right ear and talking away, as he passed by.

We politely acknowledge him with a nod of the head and a courteous 'hello', as we passed him . . . And no photo request.

The last thing you want to do, is piss off a big guy like Hulk Hogan. Renowned for making a living as a heavy-weight wrestler and usually beating the proverbial shit out of his opponents.

Marion was quick to point out his latest action. 'See!

Told you, the mobile phone is a prop! It's stuck to his ear to cover up the fact that he now talks to himself after getting too many bangs on the head!'

However, we later learned that Hulk, along with eight small people (or midgets, as they are commonly referred to) were making a reality TV show and it was being filmed in and around our hotel. So it wasn't long before we saw him again in the car park of the hotel. He was, once again, dressed in the same attire but with a blue t-shirt, instead of black. And once again with the fast emerging trademark – flip-top mobile phone – stuck to his right ear; talking to himself as he hobbled past with his limp . . . labrador and white stick. Well, why else would you be wearing dark glasses at night?

I couldn't resist it. 'Hey Hulk! Any chance o' a wee photo with you?' I politely asked. This immediately fell on deaf ears as he carried on past me, as if I wasn't there.

At that, one of the film crew following close behind him said, 'We're just about to film a scene. He'll be available later for some photographs in the hotel.'

The film crew member then went on to say that they would be back at the hotel in about one hour.

Marion was not overly impressed by the big man's presence and wasn't the least bit interested in waiting around for someone who'd spent more time on his back than Linda Lovelace. So out we went to the restaurant for our meal.

About two hours later, we returned to the hotel and there were several kids with their parents loitering about the lobby. Obviously aware of the fact that Hulk Hogan was staying here, they were hoping to catch a glimpse, get a photograph, an autograph or maybe even a shake of his hand.

So armed with my digital camera, I persuaded Marion to wait with me in the lobby for another photographic opportunity of the American wrestling legend, Hulk Hogan.

We didn't have to wait long before the big black jeep being driven by the man himself, pulled up and stopped just outside the front doors of the hotel.

Out he stepped from the driver's seat and the sight that greeted us was amazing. As he walked in through the hotel doors . . . Surprise! Surprise!

He had the trade mark flip-top mobile phone stuck to his right ear and was talking away like a demented budgie on speed . . . well, the slower version on . . . s . . . e . . . e . . . d! Ooops, forgot I need a pee!

The kids waiting to catch a glimpse of the once WWF champion, were ignored as he walked past us all heading for the elevators with his three crew members. Or maybe they were carers accompanying him.

Marion took one look and said in her eloquent Glaswegian rant, 'I'm not surprised he isn't wrestling anymore. How can he possibly wrestle! He can hardly walk and everytime we've bumped into him, he's got a mobile phone stuck to his ear and talking to himself!

Wrestler! Don't think so. He's just a big has-been that's been wrapped about the canvas more times than a boy scout's ground sheet. Anyways, I don't think they'd allow zimmers in the ring.

Now! He fights with midgets to look big! . . . Big diddy more like it.'

Fortunately, I think I was the only person present who got the gist of what Marion said and fully understood and agreed with her sentiments.

So there you go, what a let down from somebody who, when at his peak as a wrestler, claimed to be the people's champion, now all he appears to be good for, is auditioning for Vodafone mobile phone adverts.

Finally, If you're interested, I have several photos of Hulk Hogan with a mobile phone stuck to his right 'lug', if anybody would like a copy:

. . . PHONE ME!

Spell it!

• • •

I was selling off some short stories I'd written, about a 'hunner' years ago, to try and raise funds for a local charity.

A friend of my mother's contacted me and said her husband was a great fan of Scottish and Glaswegian stories and asked to purchase a particular one about the goings on at 'Paddy's Market'.

She also asked that I write a personal message to him on the cover.

I said that would be no bother and I'd send it off to her later that day.

After I came off the phone, I printed the story off and was about to write a personal message, when my mind went blank.

Now I'm great with faces, but hopeless at remembering names, and I had totally forgotten what his name was.

So I decided to call her back and I politely asked, 'How do you spell your husband's first name?'

To which she paused for a moment, then replied, 'B-O-B!'

Who am I?

. . .

For every employee who has to deal with rude customers in their day to day job. An award should go to the British Airways gate attendant in Terminal Five, London Heathrow, for being cool, calm and collected while making her point, when confronted with an arrogant, impatient passenger.

A crowded flight was cancelled after a scheduled British Airways flight had been withdrawn from service, due to a fault.

The single female attendant was re-booking a long line of inconvenienced travellers, when suddenly an angry male passenger barged his way to the front of the line.

He slapped his ticket down on the counter and said, 'I have to be on this flight today and it has to be first class.

The female attendant replied, 'I'm very sorry sir. I'll be happy to try to help you but I'm presently dealing with these people first. However, I'm sure we'll be able to work something out come your turn.'

The irate passenger was unimpressed and asked loudly, so that the passengers behind him could hear, 'Do you have any idea who I am?'

Without hesitating, the attendant smiled, grabbed her public address microphone and announced, 'May I have your attention please. May I have you attention please.' Raising awareness throughout the terminal, she continued. 'We have a male passenger here at Gate Twelve who does not know who he is. If anyone can help identity him, please come immediately to Gate Twelve.'

With the people behind him in the line laughing hysterically, the man glared at the female attendant, gritted his teeth and said, 'Fuck You!'

Without flinching, the female attendant smiled and replied . . .

(I love this bit) . . .

'I'm terribly sorry sir, but you'll have to get in line for that also!'

Cough!
· · ·

A chemist walked into his shop to find a man leaning against a wall.

'What's wrong with him?' He asked his assistant.

'He came in for some cough syrup, but we don't have any so I gave him a bottle of laxative to drink'.

'You bloody idiot.' Said the chemist. 'You can't treat a cough with a laxative!'

'Of course you can.' Replied the assistant. 'Look at him, he's terrified to cough now!'

Word Perfect

· · ·

An Irish radio station was running a competition for its listeners to come up with a word not in the dictionary but that could still be used in a sentence that made logical sense.

'What's your name caller?' Asked the presenter.

'My name's Pat'. He replied.

'Okay Pat, what's your word?'

'My word is "goan". Spelled G-O-A-N and pronounced go-an.'

'I'm getting the thumbs up from Tom, go-an is not in the dictionary. Now for the trip to Prague, give me a sentence with the word go-an that would make sense?' Said the presenter.

'Go-an fuck yersel'!' replied Pat, who was promptly cut off.

The presenter made no mention of Pat, or his outburst and continued to take calls on the subject, all unsuccessful until:

'Next caller, what's your name please?'

'Hi there, my name's Mick.' Replied the caller.

'Okay Mick, what's your word?' Asked the presenter.

'"Smee". Spelled S-M-E-E and pronounced smee.' said the caller with confidence.

' . . . and Tom is giving me the thumbs up that "smee" is not in the dictionary. Now for the chance to win a trip to Prague, give me a sentence that you can use that word in and it makes sense?'

The caller replied, 'Smee again! Goan fuck yersel'!'

Big Baby

. . .

A wee Glesca punter was drinking in a pub in London when he received a call on his mobile phone.

After he comes off the phone, he orders drinks for everybody in the bar and announced, his wife has just given birth to a typical Glaswegian baby boy, weighing in at twenty-five pounds.

Nobody can believe that a new baby can weigh in at twenty-five pounds, but the wee Glesca punter just shrugs, 'That's about average up in Glesca. Like I said, my wee boy's a typical Glaswegian baby boy.'

A fortnight later the wee Glesca punter returned to the bar and the bartender said, 'You're the father of that typical wee Glaswegian baby boy that weighed in at twenty-five pounds at birth, aren't you?'

The wee Glesca punter replied, 'Ye're spot on big man.

'Well since you were last in, all the locals have been making bets about how big he'd be after two weeks . . . so how much does he weigh now?'

The proud Glaswegian father answered, 'He's seventeen pounds.'

The bartender is puzzled and concerned by this answer. 'What happened? He asked. 'He was twenty-five pounds when he was born.'

The wee glesca punter took a swig from his glass of Johnny Walker Whisky, wiped his lips on his shirt sleeve, leaned over the bar and proudly said, 'We decided to get him circumcised!'

Bye Bye Baby

• • •

Retired police Inspector Dougald McPherson and his wife Maggie went to the Police family day fair every year. And every year, Dougald would say, 'You know Maggie, one of these days I'd like to ride in that police helicopter.'

Maggie would always reply, 'I know Dougald, I know but the helicopter ride is fifty pounds and fifty pounds is fifty pounds.'

The following year Dougald and Maggie went to the police family day fair, and right on cue, Dougald said, 'Maggie, I'm seventy-four years old. If I don't ride that bloody helicopter soon, I might never get another chance'.

Maggie thought for a moment and said, 'But Dougald, that helicopter ride is fifty pounds, and I've always said, fifty pounds is fifty pounds.'

The pilot of the helicopter overheard them talking and said, 'Look folks, I'll make you a deal. I'll take the both of you up for a ride and if you can stay quiet for the entire ride and not say a word, I won't charge you a brass penny! But if you say one word or scream it'll cost you fifty quid.'

Dougald and Maggie quickly agreed to the deal and up they went.

The pilot did all kinds of fancy manoeuvres but not a word was heard.

He did some of his dare-devil stunts over and over again but still they wouldn't utter a single word.

When they finally landed, the pilot turned to Dougald and said,

148 • • • HARRY THE POLIS

'Gee wiz old yin, I did everything I could to get you to yell out but you didn't say a word. I'm very impressed!'

Dougald replied, 'Well, to tell you the truth, I almost said something when Maggie fell out but as she always said, fifty pounds is fifty pounds!'

When You're Smiling

• • •

Three bodies are discovered dead in Glasgow City centre.

The police are puzzled as to why all three of the deceased are smiling, so they ask the mortician.

The mortician said, 'Well the first guy died of a heart attack, while having sex with his young mistress; hence the smile on his face.

The second guy won the lottery, spent it all on whisky and subsequently died of alcoholic poisoning. Hence the smile on his face.'

'And the third guy?' Asked the police.

'Ah the third guy, Paddy from Dublin. He was struck by lightning.'

'So why was he smiling?' Asked the police.

'Cause the daft bugger thought he was getting his picture taken.'

Police Questionaire

· · ·

Three police officers, a Brit, an Australian and an American were asked to explain what their actions would be if they were faced with the following scenario.

You're walking down a deserted street with your wife and two small children.

Suddenly, a dangerous looking man armed with a huge knife comes out of nowhere, looks menacingly at you, screams obscenities, raises his huge knife and charges towards you. You have a firearm and you are an expert shot.

You have a split second before he reaches you and your family. What do you do?

The British Police Officer answered:

'Well, that's not enough information to answer the question! For example, does the man look poor or oppressed?

'Have I ever done anything to him that would cause him to attack?

'Could we run away?

'What does my wife think?

'What about my kids?

'Could I possibly swing the gun like a club and knock the knife from his hand?

'What does the law say about this situation?

'Does my firearm have the appropriate safety catch built into it?

'Why am I carrying a loaded firearm anyway, and what kind of message does this send to society and to my children?

'Is it possible he'd be happy with just killing me?'

The Australian Police Officer answered: 'Bang! Bang!'

The American Police Officer answered: 'Bang! Bang! Bang! Bang! Bang! Bang! Bang! Bang! Bang! Bang! Bang!' 'Click! . . .'

His Daughter responded: 'Cool piece of grouping there, Dad!'

Lost

...

That's three times in four days I've been to the local gym.

I really must get my Sat-Nav fixed!

Chance Meeting

...

I walked into a bookies shop in Blackpool and bumped into an old relative of the family . . . What were the odds for that!

In It To Win It!

. . .

A judge in Glasgow will have to decide in a case of 'honourable intentions' whereby a man hired his neighbour to get his wife pregnant!

Apparently Shuggie Brown and his former Miss Govan Fair wife, Isabel, wanted a child but discovered that Shuggie was firing blanks.

So Shuggie, sat down with Isabel to discus the situation and after a bottle of vodka had been consumed between them, he'd managed to convince her into letting his wee pal, and long time neighbour Tommy, dae the business for him. For a nominal fee, of course! . . . Shuggie would pay Tommy.

Tommy was married to the lovely Morag, who was, by sheer coincidence, the Miss Govan Fair runner up, the year before Isabel won. And Tommy, apart from having a slight resemblance to Shuggie, was blessed with two wonderful daughters, which made him the perfect candidate to step up to the plate, as it were.

Shuggie agreed to pay Tommy £300 from his deceased mother's 'Carers Allowance' Post Office Account, which he continued to collect on.

For the next four months, Shuggie would supply a romantic, candle lit meal with wine for Isabel and Tommy, three days a week, then bugger off to the pub, whilst they consummated the arrangement. Sometimes Tommy would perform more than once an evening, depending on Isabel's heartburn and acid reflux.

After approximately sixty-four times, in various positions, with Tommy trying desperately to deliver the goods,

Tommy's wife became annoyed about the extra attention he was giving to Isabel.

Tommy tried to reassure Morag to understand, it was only a 'job and finish' arrangement, and he was doing it for the money only.

However, after six months of trying, Shuggie became very annoyed that nothing had taken place and demanded that Tommy attend Rutland Crescent Surgery to have his 'tadpoles' checked for certainties!

Tommy, the father of two daughters, confidently agreed to Shuggie's demand. However, the doctor's result of his test showed to everyone in the room, except Morag, and possibly Isabel, that Tommy was also firing blanks and could not have fathered Morag's daughters.

As it is, Shuggie is now suing Tommy for his money back for a breach of contract, as agreed over a large voddy and a handshake in the Harmony Row pub in Govan Road.

Meanwhile, Tommy couldn't give a toss! If you'll pardon the pun, stating he gave it his best shot!

Tommy has since left Morag to shack up with Isabel full-time, having formed a loving relationship during their wining and dining exploits, over the past six months at the expense of Shuggie.

Shuggie meantime, is now in the process of starting up Govan's first 'Dating Agency' called, 'Screw You Two'.

Zippety-Doo-Dah!

...

My son was standing in a queue at a crowded bus stop, directly behind a beautiful young woman wearing a tight mini skirt.

As the bus stopped and it was her turn to get on, she became aware that her skirt was too tight to allow her leg to come up to the height of the first step of the bus.

Slightly embarrassed and with a quick smile to the bus driver, she reached behind her to unzip her skirt a little, thinking that this would give her enough slack to raise her leg. She tried to take the step again, only to discover that she still couldn't. So, a little more embarrassed, she once again reached behind her to unzip her skirt a little more, and for the second time she attempted the step up.

Once again, much to her annoyance, she couldn't raise her leg high enough.

With another little smile to the driver, she again reached behind to unzip a little more and again was unable to take the step.

Just at this time, my son who was standing behind her, put his arms around her waist, picked her up and placed her gently on the step of the bus.

The young woman went ballistic and turned to my son and yelled, 'How dare you touch my body! I don't even know who you are!'

Whereupon my son politely smiled and said, 'Well miss, normally I would agree with you, but after you just unzipped my fly three times, I kind of figured we were good friends.'

Say Again!

. . .

My neighbour discovered that her dog, a Schnauzer couldn't hear, so she took it to the local vet.

The vet diagnosed the problem as hair in the dog's ears and cleaned both of its ears out. As a result, the dog could hear fine.

He then proceeded to tell my neighbour that, if she wanted to keep this from recurring, she should go to the chemist and get some 'Nair' hair remover cream and rub it into her dog's ears once a month.

On his advice, my neighbour went to the chemist and bought some 'Nair' hair remover cream. As she was about to pay for it, the chemist said, 'If you're going to use this cream under your arms, don't use any deodorant for a few days.'

My neighbour replied, 'It's not for using under my arms, it's . . .'

At that the chemist interrupted her, 'Well if you're using it on your legs, don't shave for at least a couple of days.'

My neighbour replied, 'I'm not using it for my legs either. If you must know, I'm using it on my Schnauzer.'

To which the chemist responded, 'Well in that case, you better stay off your bicycle for about a week!'

Funneeee!

...

Told my son this joke and he really liked it, so I thought I'd tell you.

Sister Marie Barnett entered a Monastery of Silence. Father O'Toole, the resident Priest said, 'Sister Marie, as you know, this is a silent monastery. You are most welcome here as long as you like, but you cannot speak a word from your mouth unless I direct you to do so.'

Sister Marie agreed and lived in the monastery for five years, after which Father O'Toole said to her, 'Sister Marie, you have been here for five years. As a reward for not breaking your vow, you can speak two words.'

Sister Marie said, 'Bed hard.'

'I'm so sorry to hear that.' Father O'Toole said, 'We will get you a better, softer, memory foam mattress bed immediately.'

After another five years had gone by, Sister Marie was called up by Father O'Toole and told, 'You may utter another two words, Sister Marie.'

'Food cold,' said Sister Marie.

Father O'Toole immediately assured her that from that moment her food would be the best cuisine and always warm.

On the fifteenth anniversary of her stay at the monastery, Father O'Toole summoned Sister Marie to his office and said, 'Sister Marie, congratulations on achieving fifteen years in your vow of silence. You may say two words to me.'

Sister Marie looked him straight in the face and said, 'I quit.'

To which Father O'Toole replied, 'It's probably just as well, you've done nothing but complain since you've been here.'

Donnie's Solution

. . .

Donnie accompanied his pregnant wife to parenting classes.

On his arrival, the room was full of other pregnant women with their partners and the class was in full swing.

The female midwife instructor was teaching the women how to breathe properly and was telling the men how to give the necessary assurance to their partners at this particular stage of the pregnancy.

She said, 'Ladies, remember that exercise is very good for you. Walking is especially beneficial. It strengthens your pelvic muscles and will make your baby's delivery that much easier. Don't rush it, take several stops and always walk on a soft surface like grass or a path.' She looked at the men in the room and said, 'And please, please, please gentlemen, don't forget, you're in this together, so it wouldn't do any harm for you to accompany your partner and go out walking with her.

'Now, does anyone have any questions?'

The room suddenly fell very quiet as the men accompanying their partners absorbed this information.

Then big Donnie, sitting at the back of the room slowly raised his hand.

'Yes! The man at the back,' answered the midwife instructor.

To which Donnie asked, 'I was just wondering hen, if it would be awright if she carried my golf bag while we walked?'

Fishy Story

. . .

A police superintendent called home to his wife and said, 'Darling, I have been asked to go to the Isle of Skye with the chief constable and several other senior officers for some fishing. We'll be gone for the entire weekend. This is a good opportunity for me to get that chief superintendent promotion I've been wanting, so could you please pack enough clothes for the weekend! Would you also look out my fishing rod and tackle box from the garage?

'We're leaving at 5.30pm from police headquarters, so I'll swing by the house and pick up my things . . . Oh! And darling, please pack my new blue silk pyjamas.'

The wife thinks to herself, this sounds a bit odd but, being a good wife, she does exactly what he asked.

After the long weekend, he came back home a little tired and exhausted, but otherwise, he was looking good.

The wife welcomes him home and asked if he caught many fish!

'I did that!' He replied. 'Lots of rainbow trout, some perch and a few pike, but I have to ask you, why didn't you pack my new blue silk pyjamas like I asked you to do?'

To which his wife replied, 'I did! They were in your tackle box.'

Ferrari's Next

· · ·

The Red Bull Formula 1 team fired their entire pit crew yesterday.

The announcement followed Red Bull's decision to take advantage of the UK Government's Youth Opportunity Scheme and employ people from Glasgow. The decision to hire them followed a recent documentary on how unemployed neds from the Govan and Barrowfield areas of Glasgow were able to remove a full set of wheels in less than 4.6 seconds without any proper equipment, whereas Red Bull's professional crew could only do it in 7.8 seconds using millions of pounds worth of highly technical equipment.

As most races are won and lost in the pit stops, Red Bull thought they had the upper hand over every other race team, however, Red Bull got more than they bargained for.

At the first practice session, the Govan and Barrowfield pit crew successfully changed all the tyres in less than six seconds, but within twelve seconds they had also resprayed it, fitted it out with a new white leather interior and sold it on to the McLaren Formula 1 team for six bottles of whisky, four bottles of Buckfast, two dozen cans of Special Brew, 400 Mayfair Kingsize cigarettes and some tasty photos of Lewis Hamilton's bird naked in the shower singing 'Dontcha Wish Your Girlfriend Was Hot Like Me!'

And from Jenson . . . Some chocolate buttons of course!

Something Smells Fishy

Early one morning, after working a long, hard nightshift, my shift were patiently waiting at the uniform bar for the early shift to make an appearance and take over from us.

All of a sudden over our radios, the police controller broadcast that a male who was responsible for several housebreakings in the area was attempting to steal a car from a driveway in our area.

Tired and weary, we rushed out to our police pandas and headed off to the address.

On arrival at the locus, the housebreaker, on seeing our approaching police vehicles, jumped out of the car he was stealing and ran straight across the Cumbernauld Road. He then waded chest deep into the Hogganfield Loch where he proceeded to empty all of his pockets of his proceeds of theft.

Eventually, soaking wet and freezing cold, we were able to convince him to come out of the Loch and placed him in the new caged area of the police van.

En route to the police station, I diverted momentarily to the city fish market, which we were passing on our way. There I obtained a dead fish.

With the housebreaker still handcuffed to the rear cage in the van, I placed the dead fish in the inside pocket of his wet jacket and hung it over his shoulders.

Moments later at the uniform charge bar, the civilian was searching the pockets of the handcuffed thief, who had ever-increasing puddles of water forming around his feet.

The look on the turnkey's face was a picture to behold, when he found the fish on him.

As for me, I kept a straight face and nonchalantly responded by saying, 'Fishing without a permit in Hogganfield Loch! That'll be another charge!'

Much to the background laughter of my fellow officers.

Bank Loans

. . .

I had an appointment the other day with my bank manager, regarding arranging a bank loan for a business venture I had . . . He asked me if I had any personal growth?

Apparently an erection was not what he anticipated as a response!

Question Time?

. . .

How come we park our cars worth thousands of pounds in the driveway and fill our garage with useless rubbish we never use?

Why don't you ever see newspaper headlines displaying, 'Psychic Wins Euro Million Lottery'?

How come they sterilize the needle before they give a convicted killer a lethal injection?

Taxi Confessions

• • •

A taxi driver was flagged down by a nun, who then got into the rear of his cab.

After a few moments, she noticed that the driver won't stop staring at her in his rear view mirror.

The nun asked him why he was staring at her.

The driver, slightly embarrassed responded, 'Well, it's like this sister, I have a question to ask you but I don't want to offend you.'

'My dear man.' She replied, 'you couldn't possibly offend me. When you're as old as I am, and have been a nun for as long as I have, you've seen and heard just about everything there is to hear. I'm pretty sure that there's nothing you could say, or ask that I would find the least bit offensive.'

With this reassurance, the taxi driver said, 'Well, it's like this sister. I've always had a fantasy about being kissed by a nun.'

'Is that all?!' She responded. 'Well, let's see what we can do about that. Firstly, you would have to be single and secondly, you must be of the Catholic faith.'

The taxi driver is very excited by her response and replied, 'Yes, I'm a single man and I'm a practising Catholic!'

'Well there you go then.' The nun said. 'Pull into the next alley.'

The driver pulled into the alley and gets into the rear with the nun who fulfils his fantasy, with a kiss that would make a hooker in Blythswood Square blush.

After the kiss, the driver got back on the road, and after a few moments driving, he started crying his eyes out. 'My dear child.' Said the nun. 'Why, oh why, are you crying?'

'I'm crying because I've sinned.' He replied. 'I lied to you and I must tell you the truth, I'm a married man and I'm Jewish.'

To which the nun replied, 'Well don't worry about it. I'm Colin, I'm single, gay and dressed up like this for a Halloween party!'

News of the Screws

• • •

So it's the end for the *News of the World* with Rupert M and his staff under pressure for the unbelievable things they stooped to just to get a story. Personally, I never take anything in a newspaper seriously, except for fish and chips. And even then, I take those with a pinch of salt.

Wooden Top

...

During a beat patrol in the Blackhill area of Glasgow, commonly referred to as 'Beirut' I came across a large wooden carved spoon, the type some folk hang ornamentally on their kitchen walls. It was lying at the side of the road, so I picked it up and duly placed it down the inside of my coat in my baton pocket. On seeing me pick it up, my partner asked me what I planned to do with it, to which I replied I didn't know, but I would certainly think of something.

A few hours later, we received a call to attend a disturbance nearby, where a glue sniffing abuser was creating a disturbance by throwing his furniture about within his first floor flat, which was devoid of any carpets, much to the consternation of his neighbours downstairs.

On entering the abuser's house, he immediately began shouting and swearing at my colleague and me.

After several attempts to quieten him down, I had a brain wave, whereby I promptly produced my wooden spoon from inside my coat and 'blootered' him over the head with it, which subsequently shut him up.

As it was, we arrested the wee dazed ned for a breach of the peace, much to the delight of his neighbours.

About a year later, I was cited to attend the Glasgow District Court with regards to the case.

My colleague was called first and gave his evidence followed by myself. On entering the court witness box, I was dismayed to see my colleague sitting in the public benches, when it was always the normal for officers to leave the court immediately after giving their evidence and being excused!

It suddenly flashed through my mind – had he been ordered to remain within the Court?

I'd still forgotten about the wooden spoon at this point, anyways the procurator fiscal led me through my evidence without a mention of it, after which the defence agent stood up for his cameo appearance and the first question he asked me was, 'Tell me Constable Morris, did either Constable Clark or yourself produce a large wooden spoon and strike my client over the head with it?'

My initial momentary reaction was to try and stop myself from laughing, then I thought, oh shit! I'd forgotten about that one'.

I recovered remarkably well by immediately responding, 'I certainly don't remember that happening, bearing in mind your client is a solvent abuser and the police force doesn't issue us with wooden spoons, or any other make of cutlery.'

At which point, out of the corner of my eye I saw the magistrate, nodding his head and laughing into his handkerchief before finding the wee ned guilty as charged!

Wedding Party

...

A fuming bride punched and kicked her newly wed kilt-wearing husband after he sat on her knee at their wedding reception and left brown skid-marks all down her beautiful white wedding dress.

Like a true Scotsman, Andrew had arrived at his **wedding** ceremony 'commando style' (minus his underpants) when he turned up to marry his long-term **girlfriend** Agnes, but his traditionalism got him into real bother and led to a right 'stooshie', when he sat his poorly wiped arse on her designer dress, leaving the unsightly stain.

After she hit him with the first punch, all hell broke out among both sides, as the well-oiled families joined in and turned the occasion into a real stramash, with mayhem everywhere!

A police spokesman said, 'I've seen some weddings in my time, but this one takes the biscuit, with us having to arrest eight guests in all and warn the rest of the wedding party as to their future conduct.'

However, Andrew and Agnes, were reconciled, after they both sobered up and apparently they had no recollection as to how the melee started.

'Aye Right Aggie! Can't wait for the re-match when she gets the dry cleaning bill.'

The Haircut. . .

. . .

A police officer's son passed his driving test and asked his father when they could discuss his use of the car.

His father said he'd make a deal with his him. 'If you bring your grades up from a C to a B average, read a page or two from your Holy Bible each day and get your hair cut, then we'll talk about the car situation.'

The son thought about the deal for a moment and decided he'd settle for his dad's offer.

After about five weeks his father said, 'Son, I've noticed you've brought your grades up and I've also noticed that you have been reading your Bible every day, but I'm really disappointed that you haven't had your hair cut.

The son replied, 'You know dad, I've been thinking about that and I've noticed in my reading of the Bible that Samson had long hair, John the Baptist had long hair, Moses had long hair. And there's even strong evidence to support that Jesus had long hair also.'

To which his dad responded, 'That's true son, but did you also notice they all had to walk everywhere they went?'

Welcome Back Sir

Along with my colleague I attended a road accident in Rutherglen Main Street.

As we got out of our police vehicle, I approached the car of the driver responsible, who was still seated in his driver's seat.

On seeing me approach in his rear view mirror, I was alongside his window and placed my hand on his door handle, when he suddenly drove off, through the red traffic signal, disappearing around a bend.

I immediately put a 'look out' call for the vehicle, but to no avail.

About a week later, we were able to trace the driver of the hit and run vehicle to his home address, on the south-side of Glasgow.

That Sunday afternoon I drove over to his home address where we saw the offending vehicle parked in the driveway.

As we approached the front door, we could hear a heated argument taking place and children crying. I knocked on the front door a few times.

Moments later, the door was opened by the driver of the car, who greeted us with an aggressive, 'What is it!'

On seeing me standing there in his front porch, he uttered, 'Shit!' And promptly slammed his door closed and ran off through the rear of his house, out the back door and was last seen scaling a six foot wall at the rear of his own property leading to his adjoining neighbour's.

My colleague attempted to give chase, but I called him

back, just as the door was re-opened by the suspect's wife, who appeared to be crying and nursing a rapidly developing black eye, but invited us inside the house.

I made her aware of the circumstances of our attendance and asked if it was alright if we waited for her husband to return.

We naturally assumed it would not be long, having been last seen wearing a pair of colourful shorts, a yellow tee shirt and one slipper; the other one having been recovered by my colleague in the rear garden, after his escape over the wall.

As we sat in his lounge, drinking coffee and munching away on a biscuit, his upset wife declined to make any complaint of assault, but took great delight in informing us that on the day of the road accident, he was in possession of drugs and that they were now hidden in the garage.

I immediately arranged for our supervisor to obtain a search warrant and meet us at the home address, while we awaited his return.

A short time later, the front door opened and in walked the suspect, 'Okay! Okay! I panicked and drove off after the bump. I admit it, now just charge me with it and get out of my house.'

'Ah there you are. Would you like to join us?' I said condescendingly.

'Just get on with it and hurry up, I'm busy!' He replied.

'As you wish.' I replied, before asking him to take a seat, in his own house while I noted his particulars.

I was deliberately stalling with him, whilst I awaited the arrival of other officers with the search warrant.

'Any more coffee in the pot?' I asked, deliberately wasting time.

'I'll just get you more.' Said his wife.

'Don't bother getting him anything, they're leaving. Now hurry up and get out.'

The words were hardly out of his mouth, when the front doorbell rang.

He turned to his wife and aggressively said, 'See who that is.'

I couldn't resist standing up and stopping her in her tracks.

'If you don't mind, hen, I'll get that. It's for me.' At that I went over and opened the door to my colleagues and invited them in.

After the search, which revealed several packs of Ecstasy tablets and two bags of white powder (cocaine).

The accused driver was baffled as to how we knew about his drug haul and we were not about to tell him at that time.

Moral of the story:

'Don't physically and verbally abuse your wife when there's polis at your door to interview you! Because a woman scorned . . . And all that.'

And finally . . .

Dear Green Place
. . .

I'm slightly confused here by the latest statements I read in the daily newspapers.

One particular paper, referred to Glasgow as 'The Murder Capital of Europe'.

I suppose in the light of the recent spate of murders reported, this title would be justified.

However, one week later, I read that 'Glasgow was the UK's friendliest city!'

What does that tell you?

Come to Glasgow, where there's a good chance you'll get stabbed but don't worry, an ambulance will be immediately summoned to attend to your injuries!!

Aw that explains it!

We're really very caring in the City of Culture!

And finally . . . finally . . .

Who's the Daddy?

My recently married former colleague Jack Burns, announced to his young wife, 'Back shortly hen, I'm just popping down to the Black Bull for a quick beer with Harry. I'll be right back.'

'Where did you say you were going, my Coochy Coo?' She asked.

'Just to the pub, hen'. He replied. 'I'm going to have a beer with Harry.'

'A beer, my Sweetie Pie?' She said. 'Here, I'll give you a beer.' At that she opened the fridge door to reveal a large selection of various beers from seven different countries, India, Germany, Japan, Denmark, Jamaica, France . . . Jack didn't know what to do, but the only thing he could think of was, 'That's lovely babes but at the Black Bull they serve it in frozen glasses.'

The words were hardly out of his mouth when she interupted him. 'You want a frozen glass, Puppy Face?' At that she opened the freezer and took out a beer mug, so frozen, she could hardly hold it. 'There you go, Honey Bunny!'

Jack looked on stunned.

'That's fantastic darling, but at the pub they give you hor oeurves to snack on and they're really delicious. So I won't be long pet, be right back. I promise, okay!'

'You want hor oeurves, Poochie Pooh?' At that, she opened the oven and took out a tray with tiny pizza, chicken drumsticks, battered mushrooms and onion rings. 'There you go, Sweet Pea.'

Jack shook his head.

'Yeah, but honey, at the pub there's swearing and dirty words and jokes and all that macho stuff.'

'You want dirty words and swearing, Cutie Pie? Well listen up douche bag, sit your fat ass down on that seat, shut the hell up, drink your fucken beer from your frozen mug and eat every one of those hor oeurves, because you're fucken married to me now and your days of popping down to the Black Bull for a quick beer with Harry Morris, or anybody else is so not happening . . . Got that Pretty Face?!'

Suffice to say, I haven't heard from Jack for some time now, but apparently they lived happily ever after

Harry says, 'Share with me!'

Harry Morris, former police officer and now the author of the popular Harry the Polis series of books, is planning to publish book number ten in the series of funny short polis stories.

Harry the Polis: Last Night on the Beat

Harry would like to extend an invitation to all serving and retired polis, along with all FSO staff, to contribute a story to future publications and allow the popular series to continue.

Stories must be of a humorous nature and can even be a short scenario of an incident that you would like the author to expand upon. (All character names will be changed).

We are all very much aware of the serious and important side of the job when serving the public. That's why the humour we enjoyed in our everyday police duties was a very important feature of our work.

So why not share it with your colleagues and the public by giving everyone a laugh instead of reading about the horrific day-to-day crimes that we see daily in the press and have forced upon us in the TV news. Everybody likes a right good laugh.

Just send stories, poems, anecdotes, jokes or tales to:
harry@harrythepolis.co.uk
And visit the website:
www.harrythepolis.co.uk

Harry will be sure to credit you with your submission. However, if you wish to remain anonymous this will, of course, be respected by the author. The main objective is not to make fun of the police but to write about the humour we all enjoyed.

So why not start writing and let Harry hear from you, we all have a funny story to tell, so why not share it?

Every attempt is made to identify and, where requested, credit the author of any material submitted and used.

Thank You!

. . .

Here's hoping you enjoyed reading through the latest Harry the Polis bumper book of light-hearted fun and laughter. As always, I have thoroughly enjoyed writing, editing and compiling this collection of short stories.

To all my friends and colleagues, past, present and dead. And to those who are young, not so young, and any who will shortly enrol for a career as a future police officer, I would offer you my invaluable experience and advice.

At all times, try and use common sense when dealing with a particular incident and don't ever be afraid to show your compassion. And, most of all, use your discretion. It's you who decides whether a warning will suffice in certain incidents, so use your common sense when you can.

Lastly, and most importantly, if you can't take a joke and laugh at yourself, then you should leave that particular job to others . . . especially me and my many readers of course!

Acknowledgements

· · ·

The author would like to extend his sincere appreciation to Peter Conoboy, Alex Craig, Richard Gault, Margaret Mulligan, David Marr, John Baird, John the Baptist, Ian Whitelaw, Tom Kelly and all those uniformed senior officers who just wish to remain anonymous (in case it effects their future promotion prospects).

Your contributions were greatly appreciated and, as always, I hope I did them justice.

A special thank you to everyone at Black & White Publishing for their continued help and support.

Contact Details

• • •

Website: www.harrythepolis.co.uk

Email: harry@harrythepolis.co.uk

Harry Morris aka 'Harry the Polis', all round good guy, is available for Stand-Up, Storytelling, Babysitting, Guest Speaking, Airport runs, Script / Sketch Writing and extensive Wine tasting!

All enquiries to info@harrythepolis.co.uk

Harry Morris is a member of the Society of Authors, a member of Equity and is registered with the Scottish Book Trust for Live Literature Events and Workshops.

Coming soon from the same author, a series of educational and funny children's books:

The Adventures of Harry the Policeman

Read all about 'Harry on Safari'

Claude the Camel

Archie the Alligator

Kenny the Kangaroo

The long-awaited first novel

BORN TAE BE WIDE

Out Soon!